THE
MARRIAGE OF
JESUS

First published by O Books, 2007
O Books is an imprint of John Hunt Publishing Ltd.,
The Bothy, Deershot Lodge, Park Lane, Ropley, Hants, SO24 0BE, UK
office1@o-books.net
www.o-books.net

Distribution in:

UK and Europe
Orca Book Services
orders@orcabookservices.co.uk
Tel: 01202 665432 Fax: 01202 666219 Int. code (44)

USA and Canada
NBN
custserv@nbnbooks.com
Tel: 1 800 462 6420 Fax: 1 800 338 4550

Australia and New Zealand
Brumby Books
sales@brumbybooks.com.au
Tel: 61 3 9761 5535 Fax: 61 3 9761 7095

Far East (offices in Singapore, Thailand, Hong Kong, Taiwan)
Pansing Distribution Pte Ltd
kemal@pansing.com
Tel: 65 6319 9939 Fax: 65 6462 5761

South Africa
Alternative Books
altbook@peterhyde.co.za
Tel: 021 447 5300 Fax: 021 447 1430

Text copyright Maggy Whitehouse 2007

Design: Stuart Davies

ISBN: 978 1 84694 008 7

Printed in the US by Maple Vail

THE
MARRIAGE OF
JESUS

Maggy Whitehouse

BOOKS

Winchester, UK
Washington, USA

CONTENTS

FOREWORD

For any student of spirituality it is Jesus' teaching, rather than his marital status, that is truly important. But his words on marriage and divorce have shaped our thinking and social practice for more than 2000 years, and it would surely be useful to know whether he spoke with the benefit of experience. As for the traditions of celibacy and the veneration of virginity that became so important for the Christian community – did that teaching come from Jesus, or from his later followers?

This book addresses two issues. Firstly, what is the most *likely* scenario concerning Jesus' celibacy or marriage, given the social, religious and political mores of his time and place? Secondly, why does it matter so much? What drives the search to find this lost wife, or the compulsion to deny her existence? Why is there this contemporary fascination with identifying her with the (inaccurately portrayed) reformed prostitute, Mary Magdalene?

Hopefully this book will help you to work out what you believe for yourself and, if it enables you to see more clearly the relationships between God and Jesus of Nazareth, our humanity and the divine, it will have succeeded in its aim.

The narrative in this book of Jesus's wife, Tamar, is fantasy. However, it is an accurate historical portrait of what would have been the experience of hundreds of Jewish girls living at that time. Throughout this narrative I have used the Aramaic versions of most of the characters' names, as these would have been used by friends and family.

Jesus would have been known as Yeshua, Mary as Mariam, Miriam or Miryam, James as Yakov, John as Yohanan and Joseph as Yoses or Yosef. The letter 'J' is not used in either Aramaic (the language Jesus spoke) or New Testament Greek (the language of the Gospels). As all male names in ancient Greek end with the letter 's', Yeshua became 'Yeshuas' as his fame spread. By the time the New Testament had been translated from

Greek into Latin for the official Catholic bible version called the Vulgate, at the end of the fourth century, the name was set down as 'Iesus.' The pronunciation of 'Jesus' with a 'J' only became standard in the seventeenth century.

However, although Aramaic was the common language of the time in Galilee, the language of trade and the military throughout the Roman Empire was Greek. People living in larger towns such as Sepphoris would have to have had a working knowledge of Greek and some of the local people might well have adopted Greek versions of Aramaic and Hebrew names for their children.

CHAPTER ONE

LEGEND, SUPPOSITION AND BELIEF

The question

No one will ever know for certain whether or not Jesus of Nazareth was married. Even if an intrepid archaeologist were to discover an ancient jar containing a wedding contract between Yeshua, son of Yosef of Nazareth, and his wife, Tamar (or Sarah or Rebekah or Leah or Rachel), it would only become a hotly-contested issue as to whether or not it was *that* Jesus of Nazareth.

The assumption that he was *not* married has been implicit in Christian belief for many centuries. The idea of Jesus as the only Son of God, born to a virgin mother, sits uncomfortably with the notion that he could have had sex, sons and daughters. After all, if he were divine, wouldn't his children be also?

However, there is no biblical evidence anywhere that he was unmarried. Certainly, there is no mention of a wife in the Bible or in any historical texts, but that proves nothing. Most of the women of those times are invisible in historical documentation. We only know that the disciple Simon Peter had a wife because Jesus heals Peter's mother-in-law (Matthew 8:14); the Gospels do not mention the wives of any the disciples. That is no reason to suppose that there were none.

Indeed the reverse is the case. Jews and Muslims assume Jesus was married. The issue is seen as unimportant but both groups deem it ridiculous to suppose either that Jesus was celibate or that marriage could ever be a bar to spirituality. The Prophet Muhammad was married and, what's more, married to a wealthy and powerful woman. His teaching states that marriage is a religious duty, a moral safeguard and that an Imam (priest) should be married.

Most of the Hebrew Bible prophets were married. Jeremiah wasn't allowed a wife by God, and there's no sign of Mrs Elijah or Mrs John the Baptist, but Abraham, Moses, David, Solomon, Ezekiel and Isaiah all had wives. Samuel certainly had sons, which implies a wife. Given the importance of the commandment to "be fruitful and multiply" to the Jewish people, the most likely scenario is that Jesus was both part of an extended family and had one of his own.

The New Testament itself calls Jesus Mary's first born and refers to his having both brothers and sisters. James, who is referred to by Paul in Galatians 1:19 as the Lord's brother, becomes leader of the apostles after Jesus' death and resurrection. When Jesus preaches in the synagogue in Nazareth and sets the town by the ears with his words, the angry Nazarenes cry, "Is not this the carpenter's son? Is not his mother called Mary? And his brethren, James, and Joses, and Simon, and Judas? And his sisters, are they not all with us?" (Matthew 13:55).

Even so, this has been discounted for centuries with the Greek words *adelphos* and *adelphe,* here translated as "brethren", being assumed to mean "cousin". It can also mean countryman or fellow believer. It is quite true that there is no exact ancient Greek word for "cousin" and it is possible that, with the close bonds of families living together, relationships could get confused but there *is* a word for "kin" or "related by blood" and that word is *sougenes.* It is used to describe Elisabeth, mother of John the Baptist and translated as "cousin" of Mary.

That Jesus had brothers and sisters who were married seems fairly certain, and is generally accepted by scholars. The case for his own marriage is still stronger. All orthodox Jewish Rabbis from the first century to the present day *have* to be married to even be considered as eligible to teach others. Interestingly, although Jesus is frequently referred to as "Rabbi" in the Gospel of John and as "Rabboni" by Mary Magdalene, these were relatively new titles 2000 years ago. The word "Rab" or "Rav" meaning Master or teacher was originally a Babylonian title given to scholarly men who had received the laying-on of hands in the rabbinic schools. It was developed into "Rabbi" approximately half a century before Jesus lived and used for men who had had the title bestowed by a laying-on of hands by the Sanhedrin, the priestly class of Israel. A Rabbi was given a key and a scroll as a symbol of his authority to teach others and he was expected to have disciples who, in turn would draw new disciples. "Rabboni" or "My Great Master" was only used when the teacher had two generations of disciples. Neither a Rabbi nor a Rabboni could have been an unmarried man as marriage was a requirement of any man who wished to study Torah.

What we do have is a tantalising gap in the information available about Jesus between the ages of approximately 12 and 30. Interestingly, these are exactly the years when a Jewish man in those times could expect to be married. Over the last hundred years or so, many theories have sprung up as to what Jesus was doing in those hidden years – did he go to India and study there? Was he in Alexandria investigating the mystery schools? Where did he go and from whom did he learn the mystical knowledge that he later displayed?

Interpretation

In fact, when it comes to Jesus' knowledge of spiritual matters, he didn't actually need to go anywhere; all the sayings ascribed to him are inherent in the Jewish traditions of his homeland. What he taught is not necessarily clearly stated in the Old Testament (although several of Jesus' teachings are re-iterations of words from the law-giving books of Leviticus and Deuteronomy) but it is clear that the driving force behind Jesus' belief is the monotheism of the Israelites.

In Jesus' day the Hebrew Bible had only recently been compiled. The texts themselves had existed for hundreds of years but they are first known to have been pulled together as a complete entity in the first century BCE. Better known, to most people, was an oral tradition that had been passed down by word of mouth through generations. This was used by the Pharisees to interpret Torah (the first five books of the Hebrew Bible) in Jesus' day. Scholars and teachers recognised that writing down teachings crystallised them and made them inviolable rather than adaptable. They believed though that, although the structure of the teaching was always valid, the *form* of it needed interpretation according to the times.

This was particularly so after the fall of the Temple in Jerusalem, when the Jewish people lost their homeland and spread far and wide. The commentary on Torah, the Talmud, was then itself written down in an attempt to record the oral interpretations of the Laws. This became crystallised in turn, and debate on how to interpret it continues to this day. There is a Jewish joke that says "two Jews, three opinions," and another that says that if a Jew were to be shipwrecked on a desert island he would have to build two synagogues: one he went to and one that he *didn't* go to. This demonstrates the importance to the Jewish faith of the continuation of debate over which interpretations are right and which are not.

An example of this might be seen in a modern interpretation of the seventh commandment " thou shalt not commit adultery". This is traditionally seen as referring to sexual infidelity, but "to adulterate" has a much wider meaning, as in two different things corrupting each other. In a particular case, it could equally be interpreted that a husband and wife who remained together when their relationship had fallen apart so seriously that they were affecting each other's emotional and spiritual growth could be committing adultery by staying together.

A less controversial modern example of interpretation of the written law might be the way that orthodox Jews nowadays adapt to the Sabbath law which says that no fire may be lit in the home (Exodus 35:3). Igniting a cooker or flicking a light switch counts as creating fire so, if Jewish people followed the Law exactly, they would have to sit in the dark all evening. However, it is now regarded as quite acceptable for electrical appliances such as ovens and lights to be put on timers – because then the spark is not struck by a Jewish human hand. This law was previously addressed by hiring non-Jews to do the work on the Sabbath day. The command not to light a fire is therefore followed but in a different way according to the times and social convention.

The oral tradition of Jesus' time has come down to us through the Talmud (Hebrew for "Learning") and the other Biblical commentaries, but also through a mystical system that was originally called Merkabah and is now known as Kabbalah.

What is so useful about this ancient tradition is that for its structure it uses an object – the seven-branched candlestick known as the Menorah which first appears in the book of Exodus. Priests and scholars were able to assess the essential balance of their spiritual teaching by comparing it with the structure of the Menorah. Nowadays this is known as the Tree of Life and Jewish mystics can, and do, still use it to interpret the Great Laws of life.

It is worth mentioning here that the best-known form of Kabbalah in the modern age, known as Lurianic Kabbalah, is not essentially the same as the teaching in Jesus' time. It was re-developed by a charismatic Jewish teacher in Safed, Israel, in the sixteenth century. He followed "the great heresy" that when God created the world, he created it imperfect, which gave rise to an external evil, which Christianity would call the devil.

In Jesus' day this belief did not exist; they followed the original teachings of Genesis "And God saw every thing that he had made, and, behold, it was very good." (Genesis 1:31). So, if we are to refer to the oral traditions of 2000 years ago we must move away from the Kabbalah of most modern Jews – and of the Kabbalah Centre – to the older tradition. This still exists. Nowadays, it is known as the Toledano Tradition after a time in the twelfth century when the Spanish City of Toledo was a centre for interfaith and study. It is not the perfect system for examining knowledge of the time of Jesus because it was influenced by the Neo-Platonic schools of Alexandria, but it is still a good tool worth using in exploring the teachings both of, and by, Jesus of Nazareth, not least because some of its precepts can be seen quite clearly in the Gospels (see Chapter Seven).

Different branches of Judaism have different interpretations of both Torah and Talmud. But the one thing that all the Jewish texts and teaching do agree on is the subject of marriage. It was considered essential for men and for women. The commentaries on Torah state clearly that an unmarried man was incomplete and, 2000 years ago, had Jesus of Nazareth not been married by the age of 18 he would have been considered a very odd fish indeed. Worse, he would not have been taken seriously as a teacher by any other Jew.

But was he still married at the time of his ministry? Probably not. There's a simple reason for this. Two thousand years ago the life expectancy of men and women in the Middle East was very different from today. A woman who survived childbirth could live as long as a man did – approximately 40 years. But two thirds of woman died in their teens or 20s from complications in pregnancy or childbirth. Jesus as a widower would have been nothing unusual.

There are plenty of other theories of course. In the twenty-first century we live in a world of easily accessible controversy where arguments proliferate, from Jesus as a celibate Essene to a light-being from another planet. The only thing that we can be sure of is that old certainties are continually being questioned. Although Dan Brown's *Da Vinci Code* was nowhere near the first book to suppose that Jesus was married and had children, it was the one that caught the attention of the wider public. The film of the book became the largest grossing movie of all time on its first weekend of release and it is now a part of popular culture. The idea of a bloodline of Jesus still existing somewhere will now never leave the realm of possibility.

The Divine Feminine

Far-out ideas and conspiracy theories have of course always been with us, often fuelled by a natural suspicion of overweening religious and political authorities and their pronouncements. For Christians, and for Catholics in particular, it is vitally important that Jesus was not married; if he had a wife, not only would St Paul's and the Early Church Fathers' teaching on celibacy as a preferred option for a religious life be open to question but Christian doctrine down the centuries would be threatened. But it's also true that today's heresy is tomorrow's orthodoxy. That stalwart of the Catholic faith, the thirteenth century St Thomas Aquinas, was once condemned by the bishop of Paris for heresy because he took account of new scientific knowledge coming from the East through the Crusades. Galileo was condemned to house arrest for knowing that the Earth revolved around the sun and Darwin was denounced for his theory of evolution (and, currently, is being attacked again by Christian Creationists).

For the last 20 years a theory that Jesus was married to Mary Magdalene has gained steady ground, even though this is just as speculative as the view that he was celibate. The Gnostic gospels, discovered at Nag Hammadi in 1945, do demonstrate that Mary may well have been a much-loved follower of Jesus but they do not offer any convincing evidence that she was his wife. Indignation is expressed at Jesus' affection for Mary in the Gospel of Philip and this would make no sense at all had they been married. The disciples might not have liked it but they would not have expressed open surprise that Jesus might kiss his wife, nor ask him why he loved her more than he loved them.

In one verse, in the Gospel of Philip, we are told that Mary was Jesus' "companion" which many people have taken to mean wife. The gospel is written in Coptic rather than Aramaic (as incorrectly stated in *The Da Vinci Code)* but uses Greek words including the Greek term *koinonos* in reference to Mary as well as the Coptic term *hotre* (also meaning companion). *Koinonos,* means associate, companion or someone with whom one spends time; the Greek for wife is always *gunay.*

But if Jesus of Nazareth did marry Mary Magdalene before the crucifixion, then she could well have been his second wife. If he left a bloodline, it's most likely that they came from the first wife; the lost wife of the hidden years.

Mary Magdalene or not, the possibility that Jesus could have been married is now gaining general acceptance amongst scholars. Nowadays we live in a secular world where interfaith options are normal. We have a wider knowledge of world religions, including those with female deities. We have female Buddhist monks and women vicars. The idea of celibacy as a religious norm is in retreat. We realise that just because women did not officiate at Synagogue services in Jesus' day did not mean that they did not live holy lives of service. They just lived *different* holy lives. There was an acknowledged Divine Feminine aspect in their lives, known as Shekhinah.

This aspect lives on in the icon of the Virgin in the Catholic Church. Roman Catholicism is seen as being anti-women in its stern insistence that no woman may be a priest but, ironically, it is a faith that venerates the feminine more than almost any other. It is as much the religion of the Virgin Mary as it is of Christ. The Church itself is seen as being the Bride of Christ. The veneration of the Virgin fulfils a deep human need for the balancing of the Divine Masculine and Feminine. The Protestant Churches lost that link with the feminine during the Reformation, and although it does have some monastic communities for women and, nowadays, has female clergy, it does not have a feminine focus for the Divine. The lack of this in the Protestant tradition may be one reason why *The Da Vinci Code* and the idea that Jesus married Mary Magdalene have become so very popular.

Paul

So when did the tradition of seeing Jesus as unmarried begin? It is generally acknowledged that it was St Paul who first implied that Jesus was celibate.

The early followers of Jesus were working with an oral tradition. The Gospels were written years later than Paul's letters. And the New Testament, mostly gives us the teaching of Paul and his followers, and their interpretation of who Jesus was. The original leader of the early

Christians, Jesus' brother James, gradually got written out of the picture. By the end of the first century, after the fall of Jerusalem, the death of a good proportion of the Jewish people, the dispersal of most of the rest from Palestine, and the spread of the Pauline version of the faith amongst the Gentiles, the original Christian Jewish sect had turned into a different faith. The Church was now taking Paul's word as final on many subjects, although he never even met Jesus in person.

We know surprisingly little that is definite about Paul, considering the extent of his writings. We do know that in the first years after the crucifixion he was an active campaigner against the apostles and their messianic Judaism. Then, on the road to Damascus, he was struck down by a powerful vision where Jesus asked him why he was persecuting him. The conversion was swift and from then on, Paul spoke with authority that came from this contact with Jesus' spirit alone. This seems little different in substance from the New Age channeling which is prevalent today. Teachings from ascended beings such as Seth, Lazaris and Abraham are redolent with good sense and a great number of people have benefited by them. But there is also much channeling which is unhelpful, to say the least, and/or dubious in its origins. The information from any psychic or spiritual source is also filtered through the personality of the person channeling it. There are enough people still claiming to be exclusively channeling the Virgin Mary, Mary Magdalene or Jesus himself to view them all with a generous pinch of salt.

For Paul, the fact that he had received inspiration directly from Jesus' spirit was more important than Jesus' teachings on Earth. He claimed to be a student of a Rabbi called Gamaliel, who was himself a student of the famous teacher Rabbi Hillel – and both of those men were conversant with the Merkabah/Kabbalistic oral tradition. It would have appeared logical to Paul to update the form of Jesus' teachings for the benefit of the Gentiles. Although it is clear in Acts, from Paul's encounters with the Apostles who had known Jesus that they were uncomfortable with his interpretation of their teacher's views from the higher worlds.

Paul is not very clear on the question of whether Jesus was married or not. One of the best-known passages is 1 Corinthians 7:3 7 where he writes: "For I would that all men were even as I myself. But every man hath his proper gift of God, one after this manner, and another after that. I say therefore to the unmarried and widows, it is good for them if they abide even as I." This definitely implies that Paul is not married at the time of writing, but it's just as likely that he was a widower as a lifetime celibate.

Later, in 1 Corinthians 7:27 he says, "Art thou bound unto a wife? Seek not to be loosed. Art thou loosed from a wife? Seek not a wife;" so we can get a clear feeling that he didn't think that marriage was a good idea for beginners or in the difficult times that they anticipated (there was a strong implication that the world was about to end). It's not clear whether "loosed" means widowed or divorced but Paul was preaching to Gentiles where divorce was common, so it could be either.

There are even some who suggest that Paul was still married. In Philippians 4:3 he writes, "And I entreat thee also, true yokefellow, help those women which laboured with me in the gospel, with Clement also, and with other my fellow labourers, whose names are in the book of life." The trouble here is that the word for "yokefellow" (which is not used anywhere else in the New Testament) is *suzugos* which can equally mean wife, partner or comrade. It is typically irritating of Paul that he couldn't use a word less ambiguous such as *sunergos* or *philos* which can only mean friend or companion.

Just to confuse us even more, in 1 Corinthians 9:3, Paul writes, "Have we not power to lead about a sister, a wife, as well as other apostles, and the brethren of the Lord, and Cephas?" Now that's also unclear because of the nature of Koine (New Testament Greek). Given the language's frequent and confusing loopholes in the linking of words – not to mention lack of punctuation – it could just as equally mean "a sister who is a wife" as not. Clement of Alexandria, one of the early Church Fathers, who had access to much earlier translations of the New Testament than we do, did take this passage to mean that Paul had a wife.

Epiphanius, a Church Father from the fourth century, and a fervent investigator of heresy in the Christian Church wrote (*Panarion* 30,16) that the Ebionites (a group of early Christian heretics) claimed that St Paul was a Greek who had visited Jerusalem and wanted to marry a daughter of the high priest. He was circumcised as a Jew but the girl was not impressed and refused to marry him. He became angry, and wrote against circumcision, the Sabbath and Jewish law out of spite.

Maybe this rejection explains Paul's tendency to misogyny, but, again, it is only hearsay. He does say clearly in Corinthians 7:25 that he has no command from Jesus concerning celibacy, but he goes on to give his own opinion – which is the one that has been adopted by the Catholic Church: "Now concerning virgins I have no commandment of the Lord: yet I give my judgement, as one that hath obtained mercy of the Lord to be faithful."

Later interpretation

When examining ancient teachings, particularly commentaries on religious texts, it is vital to observe them through the old journalistic practice of noting the six following facts. Who wrote it? Where? When? Why? For whom? And finally, Who was listening? The social, economic, religious and sexual views of the times are all relevant and need to be peeled away from the actual evidence like rings of an onion.

Of the great "founding fathers" of Christianity, Tertullian (d circa 220 CE), the originator of the idea of the Christian Trinity, the first person to refer to the "Old Testament" and the "New Testament" and the first great Christian writer in Latin, was the only one who publicly stated that Mary would have had sex with her husband. Perhaps that's the reason why he never got his sainthood.

The view of sex as being impure or distasteful gained ground in the early centuries of Christianity. It was the first monks – men who lived celibate lives in the desert outside Alexandria in Egypt – who were the important scribes. Their own views about sexual behaviour would make a married Jesus intolerable. Worse, so distasteful was the idea that Jesus' mother might have gone on to have a relationship with her husband Joseph after the birth of her son, that she was declared to have remained a virgin her entire life. This is a doctrinal truth of Catholic, Eastern and Oriental Christian Churches and dates back to the third century.

The idea that Jesus and Paul were celibate was taken up by St Jerome (331-419 CE) who considered marriage an invention of the devil and encouraged married couples who had converted to Christianity to renounce their marriage vows and separate. St Augustine (354-430 CE), having had what's politely called an active sexual life in his early years, later became a strong supporter of celibacy, teaching that sex was always tainted, even in a marriage, because it passed on the sin of Adam. He came to believe that the only way to redeem humanity was through abstinence, rather like the ex-smoker who is fanatical about banning cigarettes. Jerome and Augustine were certain that the Virgin remained just that, and the Council of Constantinople in the sixth century referred to Mary as "ever Virgin".

Later on, Martin Luther and Calvin agreed. It does rather perpetrate the idea that the only good woman is a dead virgin. No wonder feminists get so very angry about it.

The first documented official Christian Church discussion about celibacy was at the Council of Elvira in 309 CE and it appears to have been sparked by concerns about clergy having mistresses rather than a problem with their wives. The councils of Neocaesarea in 314 CE and Laodicea 352 CE ruled that priests *must* marry virgins, and get rid of unfaithful wives.

The fifth Council of Carthage Five in 401 CE was the first to actually promote celibacy saying that it would be a good idea for priests to separate from their wives and live as celibates. However, no penalties were suggested if the priests didn't take up this tempting offer and the vast majority ignored it. Only 19 years later, the Pope, Honorius, went on record to praise wives who supported their priest-husbands in their ministry. The next 400 years were marked by several attempts to impose celibacy, all with mixed results and the Church shot itself neatly in the foot with the election of the married Pope Adrian the Second in 867 CE. It wasn't until the twelfth century when the Church won power over the crowned heads of Europe that marriage itself came under its jurisdiction. Until then civil marriages were common and divorce was also a non-religious event. But, at the Second Lateran Council in 1139 CE, Pope Innocent the Second declared that all clerical marriages were invalid and any children of such marriages illegitimate, and so the die was cast. If Jesus, whose life-story is, allegedly, the basis behind this doctrine, turned out to have a wife at home – and maybe children too – then the foundation of the Church's teaching on celibacy would be rocked.

All this anti-sex theological feeling and, eventually, legislation certainly meant that the leadership activities of women in the early Church began to tail off very early on. For them, Christianity had started out brilliantly – allowing women far more freedom (whatever we may think of St Paul) than most other religions of that time. But by the time a priestly order had been established, women were pretty well sidelined. Deaconesses did exist but they were not priestesses. Where women did shine in the early years was as martyrs… so we are safely back with the dead virgins again.

Today

The discovery of the Nag Hammadi scrolls brought Jesus' marriage back into the realm of the possible and books of theories slowly began to be published, the most famous before *Da Vinci* being *Holy Blood, Holy Grail* by Michael Baigent, Richard Leigh and Henry Lincoln. This introduced the popular world to the idea that the Holy Grail was not a cup used at the Last Supper but the womb of Mary Magdalene and the bloodline of Jesus.

In *The Last Temptation of Christ,* the controversial novel by Nikos Kazantzakis which was made into the even more controversial film by Martin Scorsese, Mary Magdalene arrives on the scene again. Opposition to the film failed to notice that it never said that Jesus and Mary actually were married – only that this was an option offered to him as a temptation as he was dying on the cross. If he would give up his role as the Christ, the devil would save him and allow him to live an ordinary life, including marriage and children. Jesus lives – or more accurately – visualises the fantasy and then turns back from the world to take up his cross again, having realised that the temptation is destroying both him and all that he taught.

So how close *can* we get to the truth?

Ultimately, no one can determine whether the lost wife of Jesus of Nazareth ever existed. But we can discover what is the most likely scenario by cutting through the centuries of Christian interpretation and grinding down what evidence there is into simple piles of possibility. What you believe by the end of this book, is up to you.

CHAPTER TWO

THE SOCIO-ECONOMIC BACKGROUND

Every morning from the age of six, Tamar baked the flat-bread for her father's and brothers' breakfast, packed it carefully in cloth and laid it in a woven basket. She would add a curd-cheese wrapped in fig leaves, some olives and, if the season were right, fresh figs or oranges. It was her elder sister Dinah's job to milk the goats and feed the hens and it was Tamar's job to prepare and carry the food to wherever the men were working that day. The younger children swept the house or kept watch over the babies and everyone kept to their routine; this was the only way that such a busy household could keep up with itself.

The men left the house early and Tamar had learnt swiftly that the best way to find them was to wait outside the Synagogue where her father, Yacob, made up one of the minyon or quorum required for the morning service. She would sit on the steps and watch the world passing by while she waited, enjoying the sight of the smart soldiers of Herod Antipas's army and the brightly-colored clothing of the merchants, their wives and slaves selling their goods in the Upper Market. The Lower Market, on the other side of her home, sold foodstuffs: wheat and barley, olives, vegetables, grapes, wine, salted, pickled and fresh fish, figs, pomegranates, cheeses and animal products. The Upper Market sold pots and pans, glass bottles and containers, copper, bronze and iron objects and jewellery. In the far corner, weavers and clothing merchants shouted their wares and, behind their stalls, were the streets of the dyers and weavers.

Sepphoris was a cosmopolitan place, growing rapidly with new buildings constantly appearing and plenty of work for artisans. Tamar's family was doing very comfortably now, thanks to all the work available, and she was proud to wear three copper coins across her forehead under her veil.

Most often, Yacob and his sons would walk the three streets from the Synagogue to the workshop that they shared with Yacob's brother Reuben, with Tamar tagging along behind. This was a place of magic and danger where they used fire to turn sand into glass. Tamar had a treasured shard of royal blue glass that she kept under her mattress and took out now and again to marvel at and to hold up to the sun so that light shone through it onto the plain walls of her home. She had never seen anything more beautiful and, when she first saw the men working in blue, purple and red for a special commission by one of Herod's advisors, she sat there with her mouth open, until she spotted a small piece of discarded glass fall to the earthen floor. She dived on it like a kitten playing, but Reuben stopped her with one hand.

"It would cut you, don't be silly," he said and then softened as she looked up at him with disappointed brown eyes. "Wait." Then he had whittled the broken piece down with a rough stone so that it would be safe to give to a little girl. She treasured it from then on.

Some days, however, the men would go directly to wherever it was they were working, and Tamar would tag along behind with her basket. Sometimes her brothers, Shem and Judah, would take the basket from her and shoo her away, laughing at her, but even so she followed. If she did not they might well lose or leave behind her precious basket – the first one that she had ever woven – and she knew that that would mean having to cut and bruise her fingers again to make another.

Once the men had eaten, she would claim back her treasured basket and find her way back home. In the early days, she used to get lost and had to tug on the stola of some kind-looking woman to direct her to the Street of the Goat-keepers, where she lived, but within a couple of months she had learnt every street-corner and turning of the city and could find her way to anywhere. She tried to go straight home because her mother would scold her if she stayed out too long but, more often than not, her attention would be caught by a donkey foal or a great lady with coins jangling on her ankles; her serious little face would light up again with the joy of living and observing and she would follow them until she had gazed her fill.

Sepphoris

Tamar would have been dark haired and dark-skinned. Jewish red-heads were not common in those days, although the women of the aristocracy in Jerusalem sometimes colored their hair a light, bright auburn. It's unlikely that that kind of behaviour would have been tolerated by an orthodox Jewish family in the Galilee. She can't have been from Nazareth; if she had been, the Nazarenes would have mentioned her family as well as Jesus's in Matthew Chapter 15 when they realised that the itinerant preacher causing such a stir in the Synagogue was a local man. If she were that local, then her bloodline would have been acknowledged to have mingled with his and that was important in those days.

I've placed Tamar in Sepphoris (then called Zippori), the big town four miles east of Nazareth, where she would most likely have been an artisan's daughter if she were to be betrothed to another artisan's son. That would make her of similar social status to Jesus and, most likely, distantly related. I've made her the daughter of a glass-maker as it was a popular Jewish craft in Galilee at that time. Other possible trades for her family were gold or silver smithing, blacksmithing, working with leather or any kind of agriculture. Or carpentry, of course.

Sepphoris became known as the jewel of the Galilee; the capital city of Herod's son, Antipas, who was allegedly an independent ruler while actually being what was known as a "client-king" who was answerable directly to the Emperor in Rome. The city had been partially destroyed by fire in about 4 BCE and during Jesus' youth was being rebuilt into a modern, thriving city. It was primarily Jewish but like most wealthy Jewish cities in the Roman period, it reflected Greco-Roman architecture and design.

Archaeologists have found evidence of luxurious villas in which Jews lived, with integral ritual baths, used for complete immersion to honour the commandment of bodily purity from the book of Leviticus. The re-building of the city included a new aqueduct which meant that people could have water flowing into a cistern in their own home instead of walking twice a day – or more – to the well. For women, in particular, this was a huge gift of freedom. Sepphoris was also a centre of Talmudic study with its own academies.

After the Jewish revolt against the Romans at the end of the first century CE the Jews were dispersed and at the end of the second century a rabbi known as Judah ha-Nasi (Judah the Prince) decided to write down all the oral teachings. This had been resisted because rabbis believed that oral teaching ensured that students maintained a relationship with their teachers and that questions and comments could always be addressed. Once something is written down it becomes "the truth" rather than a necessarily appropriate interpretation of the truth. However, after the deaths of so many teachers in so many failed revolts, Rabbi Judah feared that the oral law would be forgotten unless it was written down. And it has to be said that the Talmud has done its best in maintaining that tradition as its contents are full of debate with different well-known rabbis, each stating their view on a matter – and even the losing arguments are included so that further discussion is encouraged. The rabbinical scholars who helped compile the Talmud in the first 200 years CE often earned their living by working as carpenters, shoemakers, potters and smiths. Their predecessors studied in towns such as Sepphoris, which makes it a perfect place for Jesus to have learnt his deep knowledge of Torah.

Tamar would probably have been the second daughter. The first would have married better, with a good dowry. Carpenters were not the wealthiest of men or the kind that necessarily had a steady trade. However it's worth noting that a carpenter was not the lowest of the low either. In the Talmud there is a story of a man who arrives in a town looking for someone to solve a problem for him. He asks for the rabbi, but when he finds that there is no rabbi there, he says, "Is there a carpenter among you, the son of a carpenter, who can offer me a solution?" (cf Yacob Levy, Wörterbuch über Talmudim und Midrachim, Berlin 1924 CE). This appears to indicate that where there was no rabbi, a carpenter was the person most qualified to interpret law or answer questions. Other mentions of carpenters in the Talmud carry the implication that it's good to have a trade – and Jesus is actually referred to as a carpenter, son of a carpenter. Many Christian fundamentalist sites on the Internet interpret this as an insult. It is not.

In addition, the local carpenter was also the doctor – as in setting bones and basic surgery. Medicine itself (herbal remedies and salves) was generally the women's work. So a carpenter's wife would often have been a herbalist and a healer.

The Greek word used to mean carpenter in the New Testament is *tekton*. It means construction worker but has a generally accepted meaning of working with wood rather than mason. Houses in those days were not generally made from wood – but window- and door-frames and furniture were and, with local glass manufacture, the houses of the wealthy in Sepphoris would certainly have had windows. There had been a rush of building in Sepphoris in the years when Jesus (or Yeshua as he would have been known in Aramaic) was growing up and workers on any part of a building would have prospered, even if only temporarily. Wood and stone workers from the districts around Sepphoris spent months at a time in the city, some of them perhaps wondering at what they saw: the noisy, busy atmosphere; the Roman and Herodian soldiers; the aqueduct and the Roman civic centre; the brightly-dressed merchants; the statues; and the general cosmopolitan attitude.

Did Tamar exist? Who knows? Hundreds of little girls just like her certainly did. She and her children would have lived and died anonymous lives as the wives and children of all Jesus' disciples did. The lives of women in ancient Israel go almost completely unrecorded. But that does not mean that they did not exist. But before we decide whether or not

Jesus had a wife, it might be best is to establish who this Jesus of Nazareth was and what evidence there is, outside the Bible, that he actually existed.

Did Jesus exist?

Be warned, this search is not going to be easy, particularly when we are looking at languages like New Testament Greek (Koine) and Hebrew, both of which are pictorial, expressive and highly open to different interpretations. No one in those days wrote anything definitive that would help us to be certain. Why would they imagine that people thousands of years later would want to find out when and where one particular heretic lived, and whether or not he was married? St Paul is the earliest Christian writer and he had no need to prove Jesus' existence; he knew people who had met him in the flesh.

It is fairly probable that Jesus *did* exist physically – and pretty much during the time when the Bible has placed him. But no more than that. There is no indisputable proof. Even though the Romans kept meticulous records of trials and executions, there is no still-existing record of Jesus' trial and crucifixion in Jerusalem. That doesn't prove anything either way as such records would have been destroyed after a certain length of time if they had not been seen as important.

What there is, is a plethora of contradictions. Luke's gospel confuses the issue by placing Jesus' birth during the rule of Herod the Great, which means that he must have been born in approximately 6 BCE rather than the year zero generally assumed, and therefore did not begin his ministry until he was approximately 35 years old. This fits in with an astrological conjunction of the planets Jupiter and Saturn in 7 BCE which might have been the famous star heralding the sacred birth. Halley's Comet was visible in 11 BCE, but that seems a little too early and there are no records of any other unusual astronomical events around that time.

It's important to remember here that the three wise men were *magi*, which meant astrologer physicians and priests. They were not astronomers as we know them but people who interpreted the meanings of the stars and planets. Whether or not you believe in astrology today, people in Jesus' time did believe in it. Jupiter and Saturn represent Kingship and Law and the two coming together would have been considered a great harbinger.

Only one definite source outside of the New Testament affirms to the existence of a Jewish teacher called Jesus and that's Flavius Josephus (37-97 CE), court historian for Emperor Vespasian. Josephus was a Jew and a former commander of the Jewish resistance against Rome in Galilee. Much of his work is heartily disliked by many Jews today who see him as a traitor to his race because of his involvement with the Roman army during the fall of Jerusalem in the year 70 CE. Josephus' writing is certainly full of spin, but it is the most reputable history that we have of those times.

An Arabic translation of Josephus's *Antiquities* (18.3.3) which dates back to the ninth or tenth century reads:

"At this time there was a wise man who was called Jesus. And his conduct was good and he was known to be virtuous. And many people from among the Jews and other nations became his disciples. Pilate condemned him to be crucified and to die. And those who had become his disciples did not abandon his discipleship. They reported that he had appeared to them three days after his crucifixion and that he was alive; accordingly, he was perhaps the messiah concerning whom the prophets have recounted wonders."

The more commonly-known translation of this section of *Antiquities* reads slightly differently – with the additions in italics:

"Now there was about this time Jesus, a wise man, *if it be lawful to call him a man,* for he was *a doer of wonderful works,* a teacher *of such men as receive the truth with pleasure.* He drew over to him both many of the Jews, and many of the Gentiles. *He was the Christ,* and when Pilate, at the suggestion of the principal men among us, had condemned him to the cross, those that loved him at the first did not forsake him; for he appeared to them alive again the third day; *as the divine prophets had foretold these and ten thousand other wonderful things concerning him.* And the tribe of Christians so named from him are not extinct at this day." (Based on the translation of Louis H. Feldman, The Loeb Classical Library.)

Since the seventeenth century, Scholars and Christians have been in hot debate as to whether the italicised sections were added into Josephus's work later by Christians. They don't turn up earlier than the year 324 CE, when they are quoted by Eusebius, known as the Father of Church History because of his historical writings (which contained even more spin than Josephus's works). However, the earlier Church Father, Origen (185-253 CE) states that Josephus did *not* believe Jesus was the Messiah. Origen's own work was banned by the Council of Nicea in 543 CE, so his opinion hasn't counted among the religious for a long time. However, what remains of it has crept slowly back into popularity over the last century, especially since he believed in the pre-existence of souls before birth which some see as a reference to the likelihood of reincarnation.

There is another reference to a Jesus in Josephus'*Antiquities* (20:9) which *is* accepted by scholars as being original. It refers to a James, brother of Jesus, who was executed. All the copies of the text that are still available to us in the twenty-first century read:

"He assembled the Sanhedrin of judges and brought before them the brother of Jesus who was called Christ, whose name was James, and some others; and when he had formed an accusation against them as breakers of the law, he delivered them to be stoned."

The one part of this which is challenged are the words "who was called the Christ". Some scholars say they were added later. Some scholars nit-pick about the phrase even so, because in the following paragraph there's a reference to a Jesus who is made High Priest:

"Agrippa took the high priesthood from him, when he had ruled but three months, and made Jesus, the son of Damneus, High Priest."

It's pretty clear that this second Jesus is a different person (it was a very common name at the time). However, there is no proof either way. There is other disputed evidence – people often quote the Jewish Talmud (the Commentary on Torah – the first five books of the Old Testament) which was compiled between 70 and 200 CE as demonstrating that Jesus existed. The Talmud has several reports about a heretic called Yeshu (Yeshua is the Aramaic form for Jesus and Yeshu is deemed a derogatory version of Yeshua) who ends up being hanged, but closer inspection, unfortunately shows that this evidence is flawed. It says (Sanhedrin 43a):

"On the eve of the Passover, Yeshu was hanged. For 40 days before the execution took place, a herald went forth and cried, 'He is going forth to be stoned because he has practised sorcery and enticed Israel to apostasy. Anyone who can say anything in his favour, let him come forward and plead on his behalf.' But since nothing was brought forward in his favour he was hanged on the eve of the Passover."

In another section (Sanhedrin 107b), the Talmud says: "Yeshu (the Notzri) practiced magic and deceived and led Israel astray." It would be helpful to assume that it's the same Yeshu/Jesus, and that Notzri means "the Nazarene", but unfortunately the Talmud appears to be about a century out of date in its placing of this Yeshu – a hundred years before we believe that Jesus lived – and 'Notzri' can mean several other things.

A completely separate reference in the Talmud (Sanhedrin 43a) tells of five of Yeshu's disciples standing trial before judges and receiving a verdict of execution. However, their names don't correspond with the names of the disciples in the New Testament. This could be the right Jesus but, confusingly, there is a later section (Sanhedrin 67a) where Yeshu's mother is referred to as *Miriam megadla nashaia* which sounds similar to Mary Magdalene – but actually means Miriam the hairdresser. Even today, Mary Magdalene is patron saint of hairdressers due to this misinterpretation of the Hebrew word *megadla*.

The writings of the Roman historian Tacitus (56–120 CE) do refer to "Christus, the founder of the name, had undergone the death penalty in the reign of Tiberius, by sentence of the procurator Pontius Pilate." This, from his *Annals* dated approximately 115 CE, looks promising but doubters have highlighted the fact that Pilate is referred to as "procurator" which would have been appropriate in Tacitus' day, but in Pilate's day the correct title was "prefect". That can be explained away as Tacitus' ignorance of ancient titles. But what is interesting is that if this evidence did exist, why wasn't it used by the famous Church Fathers, Tertullian, Clement, Origen and Eusebius, all of whom searched high and low to find proof of Jesus' physical existence? Eusebius was not above using spin and – frankly – deception to prove his point but even he doesn't use Tacitus' words. In fact, Tacitus is not quoted by any Christian writer earlier than the fifteenth century, which does have to imply that the original quotation may not have been genuine.

Where Jesus was born is hardly clearer. Despite what the Gospels say, the accepted town of Bethlehem is historically very unlikely – there appears to be no archaeological evidence that locates a Bethlehem in Judea at the time when Jesus was born. There is some evidence for King David's Bethlehem of a thousand years before and that's in the right place. But there was an aqueduct through that exact area in Jesus' time which points to there being no settlement, as aqueducts did not cross built-up areas. Jesus' Bethlehem may actually have been in Galilee (according to archaeologist Aviram Oshri) where there's evidence of a substantial ancient settlement of that name at the beginning of the

Christian era. The Gospels want Jesus' lineage to prove his descent from King David, so that is why Bethlehem in Judea is so important to them.

Hopefully this confusion and debate isn't too depressing – at least archaeological excavations show that Nazareth did exist, although views on how many people might have lived there range between 120 and 1200. However, as we'll see later, "Jesus the Nazarene" could have meant something completely different from "Jesus of Nazareth".

Language and lifestyle

What we know of Jesus certainly places his adult life in Galilee, which was, to the eyes of the intelligentsia of Jerusalem, the back of beyond; a place of country bumpkins who had only converted to Judaism within the last three generations. This is the equivalent to the British north-south divide and has its basis more in prejudice than in fact, but it is likely to be true that Galileans were more flexible in their faith and the women in particular were less orthodox and more likely to be prone to work with Earth energies and goddesses – and with the Shekhinah. Life and death were in the hands of the women, not the men, and there was nothing more important in a largely agricultural population than to preserve and bring forth life.

When Jesus was born, Israel had been under the governance of the Roman Empire for about 60 years. The Roman lifestyle, which brought with it roads, aqueducts, trade, information, law and rules of aristocracy, is known to have rubbed off on the ordinary people. For the orthodox Jew this was terrible. For the average Jew it was fine and dandy. The foreign oppressors might have been hated but they certainly made life more comfortable. Roman law, design and culture were more than relevant to people at the time, influencing the fashion in clothing, crockery, buildings, accents and colloquialisms.

Children will always be children and Jewish boys and girls, forbidden by their faith to create images, would certainly have run, giggling, into Roman temples to view the outrageous and blasphemous statues of gods and goddesses – particularly the multi-breasted Artemis – and maybe even daub a little graffiti where they dared. If their fathers had found out, they might have tanned the hide off their rebellious offspring but they were hardly likely to document their children's wickedness in Talmud! Greek, the language of trade, would have been understood if not practiced in all the villages that had anything to buy or sell to an outsider. Greek was also the language used by King Herod and his family in Judea, and the language of collaborators with the Romans. Many Jewish documents – including the Dead Sea Scrolls – were written in Aramaic, but Greek was certainly studied as a second language by many Jews. St Paul both spoke and wrote in Greek and a notice to non-Jews, written in Greek, was prominently displayed at the entrance of the Court of the Women in the Temple warning Gentiles not to enter on pain of death.

To complicate matters further, Jewish holy texts in the Temple and Synagogue were read and spoken in Hebrew, and aristocratic Romans and some administrators spoke and wrote in Latin.

When Jesus spoke to his friends, family, colleagues, students and townspeople he would most likely have spoken in Aramaic. But in the Temple, with the priests, he would have spoken Hebrew and in the more cosmopolitan areas – and with merchants, soldiers, officials and with Pilate – he would have spoken in Greek. This was not an uneducated man.

As Judaism was introduced into Galilee only three generations before Jesus was born, many of the country people were likely still to follow some more ancient lore mixed with Judaism and Hellenic influences. As Nazareth was almost a dormitory village of Sepphoris, which had its own priests and teachers of Torah, it would have been a more orthodox village than most in Galilee. Jesus' own teachings show that he knew his stuff when it came to Jewish Law. Even more importantly, he was frequently accused of breaking it or doing things that orthodox Jews did not do. Had he *not* presented himself as a man who was a practicing Jew he would have been discounted as an idiot or a freak. As it was he was harshly judged because he *was* a knowledgeable Jew who chose to see the Law as a device for freedom not servitude.

Marriage and women

In the light of the influence that Rome had on its provinces, it is worth looking further at the social and cultural mores of Rome and Greece, particularly when it comes to marriage and women. While Roman culture might not have been acceptable to the orthodox Jews in Judea and Galilee, it would have seeped into the collective mind nonetheless and, probably, been considered extremely fashionable. With flowing water in the cities (a more valuable commodity in the Middle East than Westerners can ever begin to comprehend), and trade and prosperity flourishing due to the foreign rule, the Israelites were far more influenced by Rome than they would ever have liked to admit. Perhaps the best analogy would be to say that if the Romans had invented Coca Cola, it would have been drunk in Jerusalem and Sepphoris, even if it hadn't made its way into the village shop in Nazareth.

In all three cultures, we have to take all the written records about the women with a pinch of salt. We can never truly know what the lives of the women were really like because all of their history has been written by men and, very often, by men who were academically or religiously minded. It's always vital to assess the filter through which the writing comes. The men who wrote about women were not the Brad Pitt look-alikes, the men who would have pulled the hot babes; they were likely to have been more hide-bound and rule-driven than the average male. A feisty young wife with her own views would drive such a scholar crazy where she might delight a farmer or artisan.

Also, much of the records we have about women – and about marriage and celibacy – are about what people thought *should* be happening as opposed to what *was* happening. It's a very fair assessment to say that no one would need to try and condemn or ban anything if it were not actually happening.

We also need to look at the most basic differences between Greek,

Roman and Jewish cultures. In a nutshell:

Greek aristocratic women rarely went out of the house except to religious ceremonies;

Roman women did not go out alone (they were accompanied by slaves or male relatives) and rarely did any shopping;

Jewish women ran the markets with their families;

A Greek woman was unlikely even to accompany her husband out to dinner;

A Roman woman could and would go out to dinner with her husband;

And a Jewish woman would invite everyone back to her place.

Roman and Jewish boys were educated by their mothers up to the age of around seven years. Daughters too were educated to that level at least, with both sexes learning basic counting skills, herbal lore (certainly enough to stop them eating poisonous plants) and manners. Greek boys were taught by male slaves while girls were not taught at all.

In Rome and in Judaism, women were at the heart of domestic life and, if their external power was limited, their power within the family was real. Greek women were "trophies" – except in Sparta where life was a lot more rough and ready, but girls were allowed to live freely, given education and entitled to own and administer their own land.

It's clear that Jewish women were a lot better off than either their Greek or Roman sisters. Even so, it's popular nowadays to look at their lives through the filter of political correctness and assume that they were put-upon and marginalised –particularly in the matter of divorce. Much of this is assumption and it doesn't take account either of the social structure of the time or of the fact that only men wrote the history of the times. Smattered through the New Testament are references to strong and wealthy women and many of them were Jewesses. The greatest advantage these women had over both Roman and Greek women was that Jewesses could own land and property. Granted that when they married, this land then belonged to their husbands but, on widowhood or divorce, it returned to their ownership.

In 1961, an archaeological expedition near the Dead Sea in Israel, discovered a bundle of papyrus scrolls, which were the personal documents of a second century Jewish woman named Babatha who was a landowner three times in her life. Her father Simon bequeathed a date palm orchard he owned to his wife and, upon her death, to his daughter. This would have become the property of Babatha's first husband, Jesus. By the year 124 CE, Jesus had died, leaving Babatha a widow with a young son. She then owned her land again, as well as an orchard that Jesus had owned in Maoza. Babatha married again and her new husband, Judanes, owned three date orchards in En Gedi. (Judanes also had another wife, Miriam – polygamy was still permitted in Jewish life at the time.) When Judanes' daughter from his first wife got married, Babatha loaned her husband 300 denarii (the silver coinage of the Roman period) towards his daughter's 500-denarii dowry. When, after his death, Judanes's estate failed to repay this debt or Babatha's own dowry, she took possession of the En Gedi land. This didn't impress Miriam, the first wife, but that's another story. Babatha wasn't an aristocrat but she was educated and her documents are believed to include some that she wrote herself.

Women could be (and were) the presidents of synagogues and, although they had no right to re-marry without a bill of divorcement from their husband (nowadays called a "get") they could invoke a divorce – even on such simple grounds as the fact that their husband refused to make love to them on the Sabbath Eve. Love itself was a moot point. In the Greek, Roman and Jewish worlds of those days, marriages were mostly arranged; when political importance was not too great, efforts were made to ensure that a couple were well matched, but affection was only expected to come after marriage, not before.

When it came to the power of men over women, the Romans and Greeks had the upper hand in a big way, which was probably the reason why widowhood was such a popular lifestyle for the women. The

Emperor Augustus was very pro-marriage and, in 18 BCE his Senate passed laws penalising celibacy, childlessness and adultery. The ruling lasted until 9 CE and continued in echo until the end of the Empire. The presenting reason for this was to impose good family values (as, allegedly, displayed in Augustus'own family) on the Roman people. Equally important however was the need for fresh young blood in the Roman legions. It was generally acknowledged that Roman society was becoming dissipated and the existence of family life was becoming threatened by a younger generation who preferred casual sex to marriage.

According to the Roman writer Cassius Dio there was a prevalence of bachelors and a shortage of marriageable women. Divorcees and widows had been allowed to count themselves 'unmarriageable' even though re-marriage for both was quite socially acceptable.

Two Roman laws were passed, the first to enforce marriage for men between 25 and 60 and women between the ages of 20 and 50 (the end of childbearing years) and the second to discourage adultery. They came with several incentives: a Roman mother of three children was allowed autonomy over whatever property she had brought into the marriage as her dowry. A Roman father of three was put forward for promotion more swiftly than his less fecund colleagues. Men and women from Italy, but outside of Rome itself, had to produce four children, and those from the rest of the Empire five children, to get the same perks. The legislation only affected the upper classes of Roman society but it had a knock-on effect, and it is fair to speculate that it would have been one of the very few aspects of Roman rule which would have been whole-heartedly approved of by the Jewish nation.

Divorce was frequent in Rome itself – again among the upper classes who had the luxury of being able to make that kind of decision. Female divorcees would usually find themselves better off re-married, but that was not the case for widows. The principle of staying single in memory of their husband or to protect the interests of their children was even given a name – *Univira* – and, if the widow had a son who was young and who had inherited his father's property, she was in a strong position as his carer. An upper-class Roman mother had plenty of authority and influence over her children, in reality if not in law, and the absence of a husband would make that a lot clearer to the rest of the world.

A Roman father had the right of "*In patria potestate*" over his children – the power of life or death. That included the right to expose his or his daughter's child – to put it out to die after birth, if it was unwanted or its paternity was in question. Unless he committed to a *manus*, which released his rights to his daughter's husband, the father could over-rule any decision that his daughter's husband might make about his wife or children until his dying day.

Despite the laws, the wealthy Romans restricted the size of their families when they could; contraception through herbs and sexual preferences were both practised – together with abortion or, more frequently, induced miscarriage through the herbal equivalent of the morning after pill (which could be extremely dangerous potions). Women who survived childbirth generally lived longer than men but they were in the minority. Marrying much younger women was fashionable both for men who had been in the army (where marriage was not allowed) and who, on their discharge, took up political careers, and for those whose first wife had died and who needed a woman to raise their existing children.

In general, a Roman marriage lasted about 10 to 15 years before one of the partners died. That's an incredible statistic to us in the twenty-first century but 2000 years ago, death constantly walked by the side of the young, married woman. The average lifespan for a Roman woman was 27 years (*The Roman Mother*, Suzanne Dixon, Croom Helm). This didn't mean that all women died young, of course, but it was no wonder that the widow capable of further childbearing wanted to count her blessings and stay out of the realm of danger.

It is perfectly logical, reasonable and rational to conclude that Jewish women of the same era lived a similar lifespan as their Roman sisters. Where Roman and Greek girls married at about the age of 16, a Jewish girl could be betrothed as soon as she reached puberty at 12 or 13. Most Jewish brides were 14 or younger and their grooms a couple of years older. The Talmud says that 18 is the best age for a Jewish man to marry but he can wed from the age of 14. So, if Jesus of Nazareth was a normal boy in any way at all, he would have married in his mid-teens and was most likely widowed before he was 30. No wonder we have never heard of his wife.

CHAPTER THREE

THE LIVES OF JEWISH WOMEN

Tamar was learning to weave. From the time she could walk, she had helped to roll the coarse, dyed wool which her older sister, Dinah, would spin with a distaff and spindle. Their mother, Judith, and aunt, Leah, wove the material on wooden upright looms in the women's section of the house. Dinah learnt to weave the year before her betrothal to Seth; now it was Tamar's turn to spin, and her younger cousin Naomi was old enough to take over rolling the wool.

Tamar would tell the other women about what she'd seen while walking with the men; this week they were more than usually interested because it was close to the end of the time of segregation, and within the next few days Judith and Leah would return to their husbands' beds. Apart from meal-times, when they sat at the opposite sides of the room, the women had little contact with their menfolk for at least 12 days each month; Judith was eager for every detail of her husband's and sons' lives. Her sister-in-law was less bothered; she would probably have been happy to live separately all the time had she the choice. Leah had nearly died twice in childbirth and four of her children had died young. There was more fear than joy for her in the return to the conjugal bed and she knew her husband blamed her for having no living sons. Under Jewish law he was entitled to have divorced her without question for being barren and, at times of disagreement often said so. "But he's too lazy," she would say carelessly. "He couldn't handle a young wife and she would bring disruption to our home."

This statement was very true. But sometimes Dinah would wish in a whisper to Tamar, when they were curled up together on their mattress at night, that perhaps Aunt Leah could be replaced by a less sharp-tongued wife; someone who was interested in clothes that had shape and style!

Leah was so boring when she made clothes – and Mother wasn't much better.

Tamar wasn't old enough to mind what she wore as long as it was comfortable. She liked life just as it was; she enjoyed the baking she was allowed to do and took great pleasure in grinding the wheat in preference to barley. Her family ate both kinds of bread but they were wealthy enough to have the softer, sweeter wheat bread. She liked feeding the chickens with left-over grain and collecting their brown and speckled eggs, still warm. She loved cooking, too, and took pleasure in browsing the herbs and spices in the Lower Market when she went there with her mother or aunt. Their own garden area was too small and filled with too many animals to have space for anything but the most basic crops, but even there they were lucky, for the city was spreading out around them and many of the new houses had no land at all.

The wealthier people followed the Roman way of buying meals from the stalls on the streets or having it delivered, and some even had non-Jewish slaves to do their cooking for them. But Judith had often observed that where there was no hearth for everyone to gather around, there was no heart in a home. The men would sit in the light of the fire and tell their wives and each other about their day, what new proclamations had been posted in the civic centre and, occasionally, news of a trial or a cruci-fixion.

There was always a slight issue about light. The house was a rambling rabbit-warren with rooms extended here and there, so that a lamp in the hearth room did not light everywhere. Both Leah and Reuben tended to be possessive of Leah's home-made tallow candles, covering their light with a basket or bushel so that it served just their family at the times of non-segregation and not the others in the next room.

Yacob would roar at his brother to share their light and, reluctantly, they would do so. "It burns no faster when you share!" he would say and then would grumble about them quietly to himself until Judith brought him a cup of ale and a honey biscuit.

She could always placate him for they loved each other and saw humour together in many things. Tamar loved to cuddle up between them both at the communal times, when Judith used to tell all the children stories about how the world had been created and how their ancestors had lived. At such times, Tamar and her father had a special game. She would lie on her back in his arms and push with her legs to break his hold around her. For years she could not do it, but one day, when she had just turned eight, her father gave in and she won the game. He was red faced and puffing but so proud of his growing daughter. "We'll have to find you a good husband," he said. "One who can match your dowry. I don't want you to go somewhere where you'll have to work too hard."

Tamar knew that having daughters was a mixed blessing; daughters were known as "an illusory treasure" and a dowry was necessary to attract a good husband. Sons were what were needed in any family but, as Judith often said to her two daughters and two nieces, "someone has to marry the sons and give them children of their own." Judith had two strong sons whom she had raised to be respectful to women. Some mothers did not do that and, as Dinah approached puberty, Judith had been anxious that she would find a good husband who would take care of her. Seth fitted the bill; the second son of the rabbi, perhaps an unexciting choice as he was small and quiet, but Dinah was satisfied – she would have the status of the rabbi's daughter-in-law, would stay near her family when she moved into Seth's home and she liked both his mother and his sisters.

In Tamar's family, as with all orthodox Jews, the women and men spent two weeks living apart. For simplicity's sake, during the time of separation, the central and left half of the house, including the hearth, were designated as the women's place with the men sleeping together in the right half of the house. Nobody thought anything odd about this; Israelites had kept the Laws of purity for many hundreds of years. The children could spend time in any of the rooms but, once the girls were menstrual, they were bound by the same traditions as their mothers. Of course, once a girl was declared a woman, she was betrothed and, usually, left the family home within a year. Occasionally, the husband moved in with his wife's family, if it was more sensible economically.

Three days a week, Tamar went to the Mikvah with her mother. Judith was one of the Rebbitzen's helpers mostly tidying up and cleaning, but also helping and advising any of the women who were uncertain about any aspect of the Law, or who needed a comforting word or touch. Sepphoris was so very modern that some Jews had their own ritual bath in their house, but most went to the communal baths for cleansing and purification seven days after the end of their period. The entrances to the baths were separate for men and for women, as was the entrance to the Synagogue, with women helping women and men helping men.

For many of the women the resumption of their sex life was frightening as, each month, another woman – in bad months two or three – in each community died in childbirth or through complications in pregnancy. Judith, a healthy mother, did what she could to hearten and reassure the first-time pregnant who had lost a sister or mother. All the women of the neighbourhood would come to greet a safe new-born and congratulate the mother. Another new life; another life spared; another relief; another joy commemorated with prayers of gratitude.

Often, when she was very young, Tamar would climb onto her mother's lap in an effort to help her hold a woman who had lost yet another baby or toddler. At such times, the other women present would hold their arms around the grieving mother, mingling their tears. Very few women had all their children living and some were forever crippled from fatal births, limping or holding their sides in pain while Hadassah, the Rebbitzen, offered what spiritual help she could and asked for help from those with knowledge of herbal remedies. She was a kind woman and bit her lip and averted her eyes and ears from hushed conversations about the power of mistletoe and chrysanthemum for a pregnant mother with too many children already and no strength to carry yet another. Contraception from herbs and salves soaked into sheep's wool inserted into the vagina were also used even though the women knew, only too well, the injunction to "go forth and multiply."

"But enough is enough," said Judith to both her daughters, on the day that she told them about becoming a woman and what it meant. They already knew for they saw it all around them – and there were no doors in their home – but even so, there were questions to be asked. For Dinah, secret feelings and a changing body made it all very exciting; for Tamar it was too far away for fear, but even so, she hoped that her parents would find her a kind and handsome man.

"I think my cousin Miriam's boy, Yeshua, would be right for you, Tamar," said Judith, stroking her daughter's sleek, black hair. "He's a gentle soul by all accounts. He'll be coming with his family to work on the priests' new houses after the Festival of Tabernacles, so you can tell me if you like him. It's never too early to make a deal if you decide that you like each other."

So, while she wove the cloth slowly and painstakingly on the loom, trying hard to remember everything her mother had told and shown her, Tamar would dream a little of a kind young man who would hold her hand in the street. One day she would make clothes for her own children; one day she too would understand the herbs and salves that Judith and Leah kept in little clay pots for times when they – or the children – felt unwell or tired. One day she would have a room of her own to share with a husband and children, and she too would make the little clay models that all the women hid in the roof or the walls to remind the Lord that they wanted fertility and health.

Women and spirituality

We know so little about the lives of women in Jesus' time – especially their spiritual and religious lives – but we can surmise a great deal, perfectly fairly. Just because most of the religious stories of the Hebrews take place outside of the home unit, does not mean that home was not of primary importance – especially in the desert where dwelling places had to be made from virtually nothing. Bible stories focus on national, tribal and state issues; real people lived in their own homes in small, agricultural communities where they relied on each other for everything and where women's activities were just as important as the men's.

The most important thing that we must do in assessing the spiritual and religious life of the women of Jesus' time is to accept that organised religion is *not* a more important or higher form of worship than prayer in the home or field. We know a little about what happened in synagogues; we do not know what happened in fields when lambs were lost or children attacked by wild animals, or in houses where a child was sick or a woman was dying in childbirth. The prayers of those all too frequent times were, if anything, more important than the rituals that have come down to us through centuries of scribes.

Until the twentieth century, the vast majority of interpretation of scripture has been carried out by men. Even the later feminist writers have given prominence to what the men thought and did, even if only to lament that women weren't allowed to do the same. Nowadays, with female clergy in the Anglican Church and female rabbis in Reform and Liberal Judaism, it looks as though the gaps have been filled. But these are only women doing the men's service; they are not demonstrating 4000 years of women's spirituality. The women were in deep and dirty at the cutting edge – and anyone who tried to tell them that what they did was lesser in any way, or tried patronising or pitying them for not performing the men's service, would have got an astonished and condemnatory mouthful in return.

Other modern views of women's spirituality focus on goddesses and many women nowadays focus on goddess worship in an attempt to address a seeming imbalance. However, both men and women in ancient days worshipped goddesses – and women worshipped gods as well, so the real women's spirituality is not there either. The Jewish women who worked in the Mikvahs, the midwives and those who laid out the dead were just as powerful, religiously trained and knowledgeable as any rabbi or priest. They trained up the best of the next generation to follow them and, although every woman had knowledge of herbal medicine, ritual and prayer, it was on their priestesses – or Rebbitzen – that they called on in times of crisis. The Rebbitzen was the Rabbi's wife. She was the one in charge at the women's ritual baths; she was the one with the say in what was allowed and what was not. And she was a wife and mother so she knew and understood exactly what the other women went through.

Historical reports of religious practice down the centuries focus on services at temple, synagogue and church. They address how people should live in many ways, but there is little about the simple, everyday worship and ritual in the home. In the Jewish faith we have details of the Sabbath Eve service and other home rituals, but the most important religious rituals that would have concerned women are those of repro-duction, lactation, disease, blood, life and death. All of these were "unclean" subjects in Jewish Law and were, if not avoided, certainly not voluntarily publicly debated by men. Time-honored rituals accompanied them, but no one ever wrote them down firstly because the people concerned were not the chroniclers of the age and secondly because they were none of the men's damn business. Had the men known about the rituals, they might have tried to stop them – but the rituals were so important to the women that such interference would not have been tolerated. These traditions, lores and remedies were passed down by word of mouth and some of them still exist today. Nowadays, of course, the equivalent of what the women did then with herbs and salves is known as medicine, and with the advent of science, much of its origins have been put firmly in their place as alternative medicine. It's not alternative, it's original and mostly it's feminine. Yes, much has superseded it to make things better, but even so, the old ways persist and every therapist knows that word-of-mouth referral is 200 times as effective as an advertisement.

Spiritual practice

The women dealt with life and death. They were the midwives and those who laid out the bodies of the dead. They needed knowledge of plants, ritual and practice – and they were not above invoking magic if the need arose. The magic ranged from using mandrake root to boost fertility (as Rachel, Jacob's wife does in Genesis 30:14) to wishing on a shooting star or crossing fingers when seeing a certain kind of bird. It also included clay and terracotta images of women, naked from the waist up, holding up their breasts with their hands. These were used as icons or symbols of nurturing in the home, whether or not there were children or pregnant women, and as images of the women who were invoking help from above. While the women could get on with their daily work, the images remained to remind God, Shekhinah or whatever Deity was concerned that the woman's prayer continued. These images had no bodily statistics below the waist, just a pillar on which they could stand. They were not goddesses because they wore no crowns, had no ornament that would symbolise divine power and they were crudely made. They represented the women below; the ones who were asking and invoking.

These images have been found in their thousands by archaeologists across Israel and Palestine in roofs, rooms, courtyards, silos and pits. It's a safe assumption that every house had one – but never once has an equiv-alent male image been discovered. Some images depicting a couple in bed have also been found – perhaps to encourage sexual relations so that children could be conceived.

There was however, one small male figure that the women sometimes used – *Bes*, an Egyptian god, was believed to protect women in childbirth and newborn babies. Having a statuette of Bes did not necessarily mean that he was being worshipped as a god, but it was proven to be a dangerous world and it was best to be on the safe side. Shiny glass or metal amulets or shards have been found in ancient homes and graves – much like the blue glass that Tamar kept under her mattress; we use whatever we love and whatever makes us feel safe to reassure us when times are bad. Then, as now, people used the "eye" symbol or *wedjat* to ward off evil. It is generally thought to be an Islamic symbol, but it represents the eye of Horus the Egyptian sun god. Those who wear it nowadays do not worship Horus, they just want to feel protected.

Similarly, today, there is a resurgence of red string theory – that sporting a piece of red string which has been wound around the tomb of the Matriarch Rachel, second wife of Jacob, whose story is told in the book of Genesis, will protect you from evil. This practice is first mentioned in Genesis 38:28 as a way of marking which of twins was born first, but both Mesopotamian and Hittite texts demonstrate that red twine was often placed around an infant's wrist to protect the child. Red is believed to be a powerfully protective color; Turkish Muslim women still wear a red kerchief on their heads during childbirth and place a red cap on the head of the newborn child. Nowadays, the red string is worn both because of folklore and because the followers of the Kabbalah Centre and its founders, the Bergs, have re-affirmed the belief in it. To the modern thinker, a string wrapped around the tomb of a woman who was, for many years, barren and who then died in childbirth would not afford much comfort but the power of superstition, tradition and both religious and cultural practice is still strong. For Bergian Kabbalists the string also probably serves as a reminder of tribe, helping them to recognise each other.

Throughout the centuries, and throughout the world, wherever there is any written record of everyday life there is ample evidence of folklore, oral traditions, remedy books, midwifery guides, charms, herbal guides, amulets, legends, songs, stories, rituals and customs.

For centuries Kurdish Jewish women used amulets in silver-embroidered pouches made by midwives; Moroccan Jewish women employed these amulets to keep vigil around a new mother, while a man outside the room brandished an iron blade to protect her. Exorcists were hired in villages from Europe to Afghanistan and metal blades have been found along with the little statuettes and amulets from ancient Israel.

Newborn babies were washed in salted oil and swaddled in bands of cloth 2000 years ago – and the custom continued as late as the early twentieth century in Syria and Palestine. It was done to cleanse the baby physically, emotionally and spiritually and to protect it from harm – and it probably had a profound effect on keeping children alive in areas where spare water for washing was a rare commodity.

It is this magic, which brought confidence to women in pain, whether emotional or physical, that has caused trouble over the centuries – so often it was deemed incompatible with faith in the one God. And so it may be; but it originated in faith and the commandment is not "No other gods" but "no other Gods *before* Me".

There were plenty of other gods... and in the Jewish world particularly, the one Great God Itself had a feminine aspect – Shekhinah. Every Israelite woman knew about Shekhinah and every Israelite woman invoked her; it was Shekhinah who gave birth to souls into the world and received them back into the heavens at death. Shekhinah is a Hebrew word variously translated as "radiance" and "dwelling place". Kabbalists and other mystics refer to it as "Daughter of the Voice". It is said to reside both in the heart of God and in the soul of a woman. By the time the Talmud was crystallised in writing in the second century CE, at the same time as the *Zohar* or Book of Splendor, a companion Talmud with deeper mystical teachings was (allegedly) first written, it was acknowledged that a man could not be regarded as complete without a wife for Shekhinah could only live in him through his relationship with her. The "allegedly" from the previous sentence refers to the fact that the Zohar was only revealed to the public in the thirteenth century and debate continues as to whether it was written by the man who discovered it in Spain, Moses de Leon, or if the book is a genuine tract from the second century written by Rabbi Simeon ben Yochai. As it was written in the Aramaic of Yochai's time, it may well be genuine. More contemporary mystics might argue that the whole book was channelled via Moses de Leon. Very few orthodox Jewish mystics would, however, give much credence to that theory.

So, there was acknowledgment in both Talmud and Zohar of the

Higher or Divine Feminine, and women in ancient days, as much as today, will have made much of the idea of Shekhinah. But the lower magic of everyday was just as important. Women throughout the Semitic and Roman world used (when they could get them) herbal remedies prepared with care and ritual and prayer as ancient as the earth is old. These included: Elecampane root, to bring up phlegm and help with tubercular disorders; Henbane and Hollyhock for pain and to help with muscle spasms, relaxation and sleep; Carob for diarrhoea; Ergot to start or increase labour; Hyssop for coughs, or Hyssop flowers mixed with golden rod in a damp poultice for burns; Willow bark for alleviating pain (aspirin was originally made from the bark of the willow tree); Poppy syrup (a rough version of morphine or heroin), for using as a narcotic and alleviating pain. To invoke miscarriage, the women used Mistletoe, Tansy or Chrysanthemum (these are incredibly dangerous, frequently causing death and should not, at any cost, be tried by the modern woman). Strangle weed was a fairly effective contraceptive, dried, crushed and boiled in water; it was also a good poultice for stings or bites. Black pepper was used for promoting stamina, easing aches and pains and bruising. It is said to help bowels and to be an antidote to fish and mushroom poisoning (in a nutshell, it expels toxins). This spice was so highly prized it could even be used to pay taxes in the Roman world.

Leaders

So this was not a world of inconsequential women; merely one where the women got on with life and used the tools they knew and trusted. And their husbands trusted in them. This reverence for the woman's role in life is often overlooked in Bible study but here is my favourite translation of the passage from the 31st chapter of the Book of Proverbs, recited by a husband to his wife on special occasions during the Sabbath Eve Service:

"A woman of worth, who can find? For her price is far above rubies. The heart of her husband trusts in her and he shall have no lack of gain. She does him good and not evil all the days of her life. She seeks wool and flax and works willingly with her hands. She is like the merchant ships; she brings her food from afar. She rises also while it is yet night and sets forth provision for her household and their portion for her maidens. She considers a field and buys it: with the fruit of her hands she plants a vineyard. She girds her loins with strength and makes strong her arms. She perceives that her earnings are good: her lamp goes not out by night. She puts her hands to the distaff and her hands hold the spindle. She puts out her hand to the poor: yea, she puts forth her hands to the needy. She is not afraid of the snow for her household for all her household are clothed with scarlet. She makes for herself coverings of tapestry; her clothing is fine linen and purple. Her husband is known in the gates when he sits among the elders of the land. She makes linen garments and sells them; and delivers girdles unto the merchant. Strength and majesty are her clothing and she laughs at the time to come. She opens her mouth with wisdom and the law of loving-kindness is on her tongue. She looks well to the ways of her household and eats not the bread of idleness. Her children rise up and call her blessed; her husband also and he praises her, saying: Many daughters have done worthily but thou excellest them all. Favour is false and beauty is vain but a woman that fears the Lord, she shall be praised. Give her of the fruit of her hands and let her works praise her in the gates."

Despite this encouraging evidence of women's work behind the scenes, we should also mark and celebrate the ground-breaking work of Professor Bernadette Brooten, professor of Christian Studies at Brandeis University Massachusetts, USA.

The website of Brandeis University states that it was founded in 1948 as a nonsectarian university under the sponsorship of the American Jewish community "to embody its highest ethical and cultural values and to express its gratitude to the United States through the traditional Jewish commitment to education". Professor Brooten's work on post-Biblical Judaism, women and religion and women's sexuality, is breathtaking simply because she cuts through the suppositions of generations. While Professor Brooten never states that Jewish women were equally publically involved in their faith, in her *Women Leaders in the Ancient Synagogue* (Brown Judaic Studies, Atlanta Scholars Press) she highlights one specific instance where, outside of Israel itself, a woman of a priestly family also acted as a priest. In Leontopolis (Tell el-Yahudiyyeh) in Egypt, there is an inscription on a Jewish place of worship saying simply, but unmistakably, *hierissa* (priestess) with the woman's name of Marin.

She also highlights 19 other Greek and Latin inscriptions (dated between 30 BCE and the sixth century CE) which have been known to scholars for centuries, and in which women are referred to as head of the synagogue, mother of the synagogue, priestess and both leader and elder. Traditional scholars refer to these titles as honorary. Professor Brooten says that isn't necessarily so – particularly in the diaspora where Jews were sometimes influenced by Greek and Roman goddess-worship. The inscriptions stating the leaders of the synagogues, all date in the Christian Era between the second and fifth centuries, and are located in Smyrna and Caria (now Turkey) and Crete. Three of the women are named – Rufina, Sophia and Theopempte. The inscription for Rufina reads: "Rufina, a Jewess, head of the synagogue, built this tomb for her freed slaves and the slaves raised in her house." Professor Brooten also comments that Rufina is credited alone; there is no mention of her husband so the wealth and influence were hers alone.

Professor Brooten also claims that references to the title head of the synagogue in Mishnah and the New Testament demonstrate that this was not an honorary title and that Rufina, Sophia and Theopempte would have to have been experienced in matters of Jewish law, as well as being teachers in their own right – and would have been counted as spiritual directors of their own community.

Segregation

If we add to this theory an interpretation of the Temple Courts in Jerusalem, we can begin to imagine a slightly different picture of the woman's role in the Middle East at that time. The Temple in Jerusalem was built in four sections – the outer court, later known as the Court of the Gentiles, where anyone could go; the inner Court of the Women; the segregated Court of the Men (where the sacrifices were made); and the inner sanctum of the priests. This is generally interpreted as being a definition of the subordination of women – but there was a gallery or balcony in the Court of the Women from where women only could see over the heads of the men into the Court of the Priests (Midrash Middot 2.5). Josephus, in his *Jewish War* agrees that there were 15 shallow steps to a balcony in the Court of the Women. It is important to point out that men were allowed in the lower area of the Court of the Women, so it was not originally a place of segregation.

Apart from Professor Brooten, all the research you will find on ancient synagogues uses the Court of the Women's terrace as evidence to look for separate sections where women *were* segregated. Certainly there is evidence in Midrash (2.5) that segregation did take place in the Court of the Women during the Second Temple period in Jerusalem (at around the time of Jesus) but only at the time of the Feast of Tabernacles which actually took place, in its entirety, in the Court of the Women. This feast apparently sparked such levity and high spirits that the men and women were segregated in order to stop too much physical contact.

Even so, the details of such a balcony for the women are not present in chapter 25 of the Book of Exodus – which consists of God-given instructions for the design of the tabernacle which later became the Temple. The rabbis had to do a lot of justifying for it in Talmud, using the section in the book of Zechariah which says that the Lord shall mourn, every family apart; and the family of the House of David apart, and their wives apart (Zechariah 12.12). The rabbis used this to justify the claim that it was much more important to separate men and women if they were engaged in rejoicing and therefore more prone to the "evil inclination"(Talmud Sukk 52a). As arguments go, this is pretty feeble.

Professor Brooten's suggestions – that women may have been more involved in Jewish religious ritual than is generally assumed nowadays – are interesting and relevant. But I also like an unconventional but contemporary Jewish interpretation of why women in synagogues *should* be elevated and separated from men. Some orthodox Jewish men truly believe that women are born at a higher spiritual level than men and their placing on the balcony acknowledges both this and the fact that they have no need to participate in the men's service, being already elevated to the level of Shekhinah. If that should be the case then women have no grounds whatsoever for grumbling about the additional work of participating in the church or synagogue service.

CHAPTER FOUR

MARRIAGE IN THE ANCIENT WORLD – RULES AND REGULATIONS

Leah was pregnant again. She spent her time alternating between hope and despair and both Judith and the women at the Mikvah had a hard time with her mood swings. She drank copious amounts of raspberry and nettle teas to strengthen her body, and she prayed endlessly: this time it must be a son; this time the child must live; this time she must come through without the pain and horror of the previous pregnancies. The women did all they could to help her, even renewing the images hidden in the roof of the house. Judith made sure that Leah rested in the afternoons – giving more work to all of the children and chiding her own sons if they resisted doing "women's work".

Dinah was spending more and more time at Seth's home and the wedding plans took up almost as much time as nurturing Leah in the last months of her pregnancy.

Tamar observed it all, doing what she could to help, bathing her aunt's face and hands with lavender water and running errands. She found the beauty of the blue glass a great comfort. She would take it out from under her bed at night and fondle it and whisper to it when Leah's crying kept her awake. It was not an easy pregnancy but it did, this time, go to term.

As Leah struggled in labour the men stayed away, knowing this was women's work and not wanting to be in the way. The midwives did all they could – Jewish law was clear that the mother's life was sacrosanct until the baby was visible. Once the child was seen to be alive, there were times when choices had to be made, but by that time the die was usually cast. After three days of torment, the women sacrificed Leah's son inside her in order to save the terrified woman's life, even though she cursed them bitterly as they did so.

There would be no more children; Leah barely recovered, a shadow of herself and in constant pain. She was frighteningly humbled and helpless, and a dreadful quietness spread through the house for there was, at last, talk of divorce. It was not that she was not a good wife, Reuben argued with Yacob and the Rabbi Simeon, but he needed sons. And Leah could not give them to him. Hadassah, the Rebbitzen, sat with Leah while the men talked, but the defeated woman turned her face to the wall and would not speak to her.

"What will happen to her if you release her?" Judith said to her brother-in-law. Judith was so angered and frightened at what she was hearing that she had refused to cook a meal – in itself a defiance that could be punished by threat of divorce. But Judith was pregnant herself, the mother of two fine sons and a fine, good and powerful woman; no sensible man would consider letting her go.

"She can go back to her family in Nazareth," said Reuben. "Her brothers can take her in."

"She will die within the year," said Judith flatly. "She may die within the week; there is no hope left in her. You could at least let her decide between life and death in her own home with her own daughters."

She took her own husband's hand and knelt at his feet. "For the family's sake," she said. "There would be too much pain. Give it a year. Just one more year."

"But Leah can have no more children," said Reuben stubbornly, as Yacob shook his head and patted his wife's hand. Yacob was head of the family but did not want to have to decide on this issue.

"What about your daughters?" said Judith. "Do they go away with her? Or stay with you? They will need dowries; you can't cast them away and Leah's brothers have no responsibility for them."

"They will stay here," said Reuben. "My new wife will care for them."

"Have you an eye for a woman?" said Yacob as his wife threw up her hands in despair.

"Yes," said Reuben. "Your daughter, Tamar."

"Tamar?" Judith and Yacob were stunned.

"Yes, a man is permitted to marry his niece and it will ensure that the family does not have a stranger coming in and disrupting us. My daughters love Tamar and there will be no question of a dowry which will help you both after what you have given for Dinah's betrothal."

"But Tamar is not yet at puberty," said Judith, stalling for time to think.

"She is on the verge," said Reuben. "I can wait a few months. If you prefer I will take her as a second wife and not divorce Leah. It is allowed."

"It would be a solution," said Yacob to his wife. He was frowning, but Reuben was right; the law allowed for a man to marry his brother's daughter. And there would be far less trouble.

"But we women have so much work to do already!" said Judith, putting aside her emotions for the moment for she knew they would not influence the men. "Tamar works all the time. If she replaced Leah there would be even more work to do. She is very young – and Reuben, I had hoped for a younger man for her."

"An older man with experience can be a good thing," said Yacob. He was warming to the idea. "We will consider it."

With that, both Reuben and Judith knew that the matter was closed for the moment. When Yacob did rule on a family matter, his ruling was final – but it was never given without a good night's sleep, discussion with the Minyon at the Synagogue and some serious contemplation.

Judith said nothing to Tamar and nothing to Leah, who lay white and silent on a mattress in the store room. For Leah, she could do nothing but rub salves on the suffering woman's hands and face, check the diminishing bleeding and offer food or drink. But, for her daughter's future, she would fight.

That night she calculated by the moon the likelihood of it being the time of separation for the women of her cousin's family in nearby

Nazareth. This was the time when the women of the family would be menstruating (women living together would menstruate at the same time, with the obvious changes and adaptation of childbirth taken into account). Judith knew which Moon-phase meant menstruation for her cousin for she knew it as well as she knew her own: those times were when the women would gather together if they had secrets to tell or needed help outside of the rule of the men. The moon phase was encouraging and Judith smiled to herself when the calculation was made. She would be able to ask advice from those she trusted. The following morning once Tamar had come home from taking the men's breakfast, she instructed Dinah, in a tone that would brook no argument, to take care of Leah and her daughters and to finish the weaving in hand. Then she made her younger daughter put on the sandals that meant a long journey was ahead, and set out with her to walk the four miles to Nazareth.

Marriage

Marriage was required in the Jewish world of Jesus' time. Heartless as Reuben might appear to us, it was a religious duty to have sons – and both sexes knew that. Even as late as Tudor times in England, King Henry VIII was so concerned about the lack of a male heir that he defied the Pope to marry Anne Boleyn. And when she too could not carry a boy child, she was executed on trumped-up charges. Male children are still valued over girls in many places in the world today, and there are substantiated stories both of selective abortion in Western countries and of baby daughters being exposed to die in countries such as China where there is still a one-child rule. In Tamar's time, if a man had no son from his first wife, Jewish law even allowed him to sell a precious scroll of the Torah in order to find the money to wed a wife who could bear him children.

We can see Biblical evidence of the women's constant fear of being childless in the stories of the Biblical Matriarchs. Sarah and Rachel both gave their handmaidens to their husbands in order that they could have sons. Rachel even said to her husband Jacob, "Give me sons or I shall die." (Genesis 30:1) This was despite the fact (or, more likely, because of it) that Rachel's sister, Leah, Jacob's first wife, was the mother of six sons.

Polygamy was perfectly permitted in Biblical times, but it was not a particularly common occurrence. It was formally forbidden for Ashkenazi Jews only as late as the twelfth century. There has never been any ruling for Sephardi Jews so, technically, if they lived in a land where polygamy was permitted, Sephardi Jewish men could still have more than one wife. In the Middle Ages, the Jewish nation split into two groups. The Ashkenazim lived in Eastern Europe (the term comes from a Hebrew word for Germany) and they now include Jews from Northern and Eastern Europe and their descendants from émigrés to America. The Sephardim (from a Hebrew word for Spain), lived in the Iberian peninsula and the term now includes Jews of Mediterranean, Balkan, Aegean and Middle Eastern origins. There are several differences in ritual and practice between the two groups, but both have always recognized the validity and authority of the other's rabbinical rulings.

In Tamar's day, as with most cultures, Jewish marriages were arranged by parents, generally within their own wider family, or where a link with another family would be advantageous and, although efforts were made to ensure that the young couple were compatible, the luxury of love was not considered important. Sons and daughters were betrothed at puberty and married in the following year. For a young boy to resist this and refuse to marry was almost unheard of. Only if the boy's parents thought along the same lines as their son could it even be considered – and they would have to be members of a like-minded group, such as the Essenes, for it to happen without extreme censure within the community. The only men who could choose not to marry were either Essenes or Nazarites. It is unlikely that Jesus was either.

There is nothing in the Hebrew Bible that actually says "you must get married or you're in trouble" but Jewish belief that marriage is vital for fulfilment is not only based on the well-known command to "be fruitful and multiply" (Genesis 1:22) but also on the phrase, "it is not good that a man should be alone; I shall make a helper [ayzer – one who nurtures] for him...therefore shall a man leave his father and mother and shall cleave to his wife, and they shall become one flesh." (Genesis 2:18). Talmud puts it a little more succinctly: "He who has no wife is no man" (Yebamot 63a). The value of marriage for a man is most frequently emphasised in Jewish texts (this is unsurprising given that all the texts are written by male scholars) but throughout the Talmud great attention is placed on the rights of the wives – from economic to sexual. A man is expected to love his wife as he loves himself and to honor her more than he honors himself (Yebamot 62b).

Marriage and children

It's probably worth looking at the Talmud more deeply here. Remember, this is essentially a series of debates on the written Law of the Torah, the first five books of the Bible. Talmud comes in two versions, the definitive version usually being thought of as being the one compiled in Babylonia, which is known, unsurprisingly, as the Babylonian Talmud. This is about 6000 pages long and written in an Eastern form of Aramaic. The second version, the Palestinian Talmud, is around 2000 pages long and, although written in Western Aramaic, includes quite a few Koine/Greek words.

Talmud wasn't completely finished until the sixth century CE, but it is still the most authoritative source we have to examine life in Jesus' time, simply because the customs and laws had remained the same for centuries. The Talmud comes in two parts: the Mishnah and the Gemara. Mishnah, which is the one that concerns us – the written version of which dates back to the second century – is the section that focuses on religious, political and civil laws and traditions dating back to 450 BCE.

Gemarah came along later because it turned out that Mishnah was too complicated or inappropriate for many people to understand or follow as humanity developed and the Jewish nation dispersed throughout the world, following the fall of the Temple in 70 CE. New interpretations were required for emerging lifestyles. Gemara is much longer than Mishnah. Both sections have two sections of their own: Halachah – which deals with legal questions and the decisions made – and Haggadah which carries stories that illustrate Halachah.

As an example of how it all works, Torah has the story of the Exodus from Egypt and contains the command to celebrate the Passover. The Halachah of Talmud debates *how* the Passover should be celebrated – with rules on cleaning the house and the appropriate food to be eaten – while Haggadah sets out the prayers, songs and stories to be used during the Passover service.

In addition to all this, Talmud comes in six sections with their own sub-sections. The sections are:

Zera'im (Seeds): Daily prayer rituals and agricultural law.

Mo'ed (Festival): Rituals, ceremonies, prohibitions, fasting in relation to the Sabbath and the Jewish festivals.

Nashim (Women): Married life, Nazarite vows and divorce.

Neziqim (Damages): Criminal law, courts and punishment.

Qodashim (Holiness): Rituals of the Temple in Jerusalem

Tohorot (Purifications): Ritual purity of people, foods, vessels and lifestyle.

Here are some of the Talmudic extracts about marriage:

"Rabbi Tanhum ben R. Hanilai said, 'Any man who lives without a wife lives without happiness, without blessing and without good'. 'Without happiness' as it is written: 'And you shall…rejoice with your household' (Deuteronomy 14:26). 'Without blessing' as it is written 'that a blessing may rest upon your home' (Ezekiel 44:30). 'Without good' as it is written 'It is not good for man to be alone' Genesis 2:18).

"In the West they say; 'without a help, without wisdom, without

Torah, without a wall, without a dwelling.' 'Without a help' as it is written 'I will make a fitting helper for him' (Genesis 2:18). 'Without wisdom' as it is written 'Truly I cannot help myself: I have been deprived of resourcefulness" (Job 6:13). 'Without a wall' as it is written 'a woman encircles a man' (Jeremiah 31:21). 'Without a dwelling' as it is written 'You will know that all is well in your tent; when you visit your home you will never fail.' (Job 5:24)." (Yevamot 61B–64A II)

(The above appears more to be a reference to houses rather than wives but this excerpt is generally acknowledged by scholars throughout the centuries to refer to the creation of "households" which involved husband and wife together).

"A man should not cease from procreation unless he has children. The School of Shammai says two boys. The school of Hillel says a boy and a girl as it is written 'Male and Female he created them.' (Gen 5:2)" Yevamot 61B-64A (I)

The Talmudic commentary says:

"But if he has children, he may abstain from procreation, but he may not abstain from having a wife. This is a help to Rav Nahman who said in the name of Shmuel, 'Even if a man has several children, he is forbidden to live without a wife, as it is said: 'It is not good for a man to be alone' (Gen 2:18)

"But some say that if he has children he may abstain both from procreation and from having a wife... No. If he has no children he marries a woman capable of bearing children. But if he has children, he can marry a woman not capable of bearing children... he may sell a Torah scroll in order to marry a woman capable of bearing children.

"Our rabbis taught: One who loves his wife like himself and honors her more than himself and raises his sons and daughters along the straight path and marries them close to their reaching puberty, about him Scripture says 'and you will know that your tent is on peace.'

"One who loves his neighbours and draws his relatives close and marries the daughter of his sister and loans a sela to a poor person in need, about him Scripture says 'Then when you will call, the Lord will answer; when you will cry He will say, *Here I am.* (Isa 58:9)." Yevamot 61B-64A (IV).

Sex is also covered in Talmudic teaching – and it is the woman's right, not the man's. Her husband is required to make love to her regularly – and to ensure that sex is pleasurable for her. The woman's right to sexual intercourse is called *mitzvat onah*, (a commandment to be performed at set times) and it is one of a wife's three basic rights. The others are food and clothing. Talmud, Eruvin 100b states: "A man is forbidden to compel his wife to have marital relations…" Rabbi Joshua ben Levi similarly stated: "Whosoever compels his wife to have marital relations will have unworthy children."

A woman may withhold sex from her husband for good reason – but not as a form of punishment. If she does, the husband may divorce her.

The Ketubot 61b section of Talmud even lays down the amount of sexual obligation a man has according to his occupation. A scholar is only required to make love to his wife on Sabbath Eve (Friday night) – but if he refuses to do that, his wife can divorce him. This right to divorce a man is a two-edged sword however as divorce was granted on two levels – civil and religious. The religious divorce or *get* can only be applied for by the husband and if he refuses to do that, then an orthodox Jewish woman cannot marry again.

Judaism teaches that the bodily pleasures of eating and of sex are to be enjoyed as much as reasonably possible. Abstaining from pleasure is seen as an ungrateful rejection of God's blessings; the Talmud even says we will be accountable in the life to come for all our failures to enjoy pleasure on Earth.

"There must be close bodily contact during sex. This means that a husband must not treat his wife in the manner of the Persians, who perform their marital duties in their clothes". (Ketubot 48a)

For Jewish mystics, the great Kabbalistic text *The Zohar* also emphasises the importance of marriage, going so far as to state that no man is complete without a wife because she is the living representative of Shekhinah (the feminine aspect of God) in his life and when he is apart from her, God sends the spiritual Shekhinah with him to keep him safe. When he is home with her, Shekhinah is automatically there, because of his wife's presence (Zohar, Conjugal Life: 147-187).

The importance of the woman's presence to light the Sabbath candles on a Friday night is emphasised in the Zohar in the telling of how Rebekah brought the light back into Abraham and Isaac's tent after the death of Sarah:

When a man is at home the principal element of his home is his wife, for the Shekhinah does not leave the home as long as his wife is there. For we have learned from the verse "Isaac brought her into the tent of Sarah, his mother," (Genesis 24:67) that the lamp was kindled... Why? Because the Shekhinah came into the home. (Zohar, Conjugal Life: 168).

Nazarites

It is true that the Talmud was not put together until after the life of Jesus – but it had been a long time in the making and it certainly reflected the views of 100 years before it was written. For Jesus not to have been married would have meant he went against all the views of the age; he would have been a pariah – and not taken seriously as a teacher.

What seems to be the most obvious alternative was that he was a Nazarite. This is the name given to people who take a particular vow of abstention and separation and is described in the book of Numbers. The word is so similar to Nazarene that it has often been suggested that Jesus was a Nazarite rather than a person of Nazareth. As always, the complication is in the translation. The Hebrew root of the two words is quite

different. The town, transliterated, would be "Nats-raht" which means
branch or shoot, while the vow would be "nah-zear", meaning promise.
Isaiah 11:1 says: "Then a shoot will spring from the stem of Jesse, and a
Branch from his roots will bear fruit" and Christian scholars have always
taken that to refer to Jesus' coming from the town of the shoot, Nazareth.
However, the Nazarite vow from the Hebrew Bible is worth looking
at in full:

> "And the Lord spake unto Moses, saying, Speak unto the children of
> Israel, and say unto them, When either man or woman shall go apart
> to vow a vow of a Nazarite, to separate unto the Lord: He shall
> separate from wine and strong drink, and shall drink no vinegar of
> wine, or vinegar of strong drink, neither shall he drink any liquor of
> grapes, nor eat moist grapes, or dried.
>
> All the days of his separation shall he eat nothing that is made of
> the vine tree, from the kernels even to the husk.
>
> All the days of the vow of his separation there shall no razor come
> upon his head: until the days be fulfilled, in which he separates unto
> the Lord, he shall be holy, and shall let the locks of the hair of his head
> grow.
>
> All the days that he separates unto the Lord he shall come at no
> dead body. He shall not make himself unclean for his father, or for his
> mother, for his brother, or for his sister, when they die: because the
> consecration of his God is upon his head.
>
> All the days of his separation he is holy unto the Lord."(Numbers
> 6:1)

There is more detail after this, but it is about the sacrifices that the
Nazarite needs to make to end his or her vow. Numbers goes on to say
"when the days of his separation are fulfilled: he shall be brought unto the
door of the tabernacle of the congregation" showing that, as a general
rule, a Nazarite vow was not for life; it was expected to be of a particular

duration. However (and I'm afraid there is always a however) there are definite instances of Nazarites making vows for life – and even of parents making a Nazarite vow for their children. Both Samson (whose power ended when Delilah cut his hair) and the Prophet Samuel were sworn as Nazarites by their mothers before birth.

There's further evidence of this in Judges 13:6-7:

"Then the woman went to her husband and told him, 'A man of God came to me. He looked like an angel of God, very awesome. I didn't ask him where he came from, and he didn't tell me his name. But he said to me, "You will conceive and give birth to a son. Now then, drink no wine or other fermented drink and do not eat anything unclean, because the boy will be a Nazarite of God from birth until the day of his death."

It would appear from the Talmud, the Jewish commentary on the Law, that most Nazarite vows were of short duration – perhaps a month or so. And such a vow of separation would mean not co-habiting with an existing husband or wife – but it doesn't necessarily mean not getting married in the first place. A couple could agree to take a Nazarite vow together for some time; but certainly if one of them took the vow without consulting the other, it would be grounds for divorce.

So was Jesus a Nazarite? Pictures always show him with long hair – but there are no pictures that were actual portraits, so that counts for nothing (and also Jesus as depicted always has a very neat beard – and Nazarites wouldn't trim their beards). However, Jesus definitely drank wine; we would not have the Christian communion service if he didn't. And if he were a Nazarite, he was hardly likely to attend a wedding at Cana, let alone turn water into wine. In Luke 7:34 he owns up to supping the odd glass of plonk: "The Son of man is come eating and drinking; and ye say, Behold a gluttonous man, and a winebibber, a friend of publicans and sinners!" (ditto Matthew 11:19).

This is particularly interesting in contrast with the life of John the Baptist. The angel that announces his birth to his mother Elizabeth in Luke 1:15 says "he shall be great in the sight of the Lord, and shall drink neither wine nor strong drink; and he shall be filled with the Holy Ghost, even from his mother's womb." This sounds very much like a pre-birth Nazarite contract.

As a Nazarite, Jesus would also be prohibited from associating in any way with death – and the Gospels are clear that he raised at least three people from the dead. Most people have heard of the raising of Lazarus from the dead (John 11:43) and you could just about get away with that one because there is no mention of Jesus touching Lazarus; he could have given his orders from a sufficient distance. But there is also Jairus' daughter in Mark 5 and Luke 8:54 where Jesus takes the dead girl by the hand to bring her back to life. The third resurrection miracle is the widow's son in Luke 7:14: "And he came and touched the bier: and they that bare him stood still. And he said, Young man, I say unto thee, Arise. And he that was dead sat up, and began to speak. And he delivered him to his mother."

If Jesus were a Nazarite, then he must have completed the vow before beginning his ministry. It is possible that he could have made the vow at 13 and not married and completed it at 30 – perhaps he went to John the Baptist for baptism as a symbol of that new life. And then he would have run out of reasons for not getting married. So that is about the best case we have so far for his marrying late – and perhaps for marrying Mary Magdalene. However, it is still most unlikely.

Interestingly there *is* evidence that St Paul took the Nazarite vow, for a while at least. Nazarites would shave their heads before making their vow so that all their later growth of hair was evidence of the contract, and in Acts 18:18 it says: "And Paul after this tarried there yet a good while, and then took his leave of the brethren, and sailed thence into Syria, and with him Priscilla and Aquila, having shorn his head in Cenchrea; for he had a vow." Later, in Acts 21:26, it records how he ends that vow.

It is also quite possible that the Virgin Mary was a Nazarite – that would be the one thing that explained the idea of perpetual virginity (although not the brothers and sisters of Jesus, unless Joseph had been married before). However, if she abjured wine, she would hardly have been likely to have insisted that her son turned water into wine at the Wedding at Cana, and if John the Baptist's pre-birth Nazarite vow was relevant, then hers would have been mentioned too. After all, it would have made the Virgin Birth undeniable.

Essenes

The possibility of Jesus being an Essene is even more complicated. I once wrote a novel about a fictional female cousin of Jesus in which I made him a celibate and an Essene. It was just about possible that Jesus had lived and learnt with the Essenes, but there was much of their teaching which he had to reject in order to be who he was. In the book, I had him living and working almost as a part-time Essene. This was possible, but as only the inner core of the Essene groups in Judea in those days was celibate, it took a bit of shoehorning to get it all to fit.

Quite frankly, there's a lot of bunk about the Essenes floating around nowadays. Most of it is very well-meaning and all of it is based on some aspect of localised evidence. There's even a modern-day order of the Nazorean Essenes, a Buddhist branch of "original Christianity". However, much of it is supposition at the least. There definitely were such people as Essenes and some sparing details about them are recorded by Flavius Josephus in his *Jewish War* and *Antiquities*, by Pliny the Elder (approx 23 CE to 79 CE) in his *Natural History* and by Philo of Alexandria. Philo was a Jewish mystic who lived approximately between 15 BCE and 50 CE who was incredibly influential in interpreting Jewish Law through Greek philosophy. He compared the Essenes with the Therapeutae, a single sex, segregated group of men and women who lived a monastic life outside Alexandria. The way in which the Therapeutae are described in Philo's writings emphasises that this was a practice that was regarded as most unusual, if not actually unknown, within Judaism. This is also where the general assumption that Essenes were celibate and lived in closed communities comes from, although both Philo and Josephus also make it clear that Essenes also lived in towns throughout "Palestinian Syria" and that more than 4000 of them existed.

The idea that the Essenes' primary settlement was at Qumran by the Dead Sea comes from Pliny's work as he locates them "on the west side of the Dead Sea, away from the coast". Archaeologists have now come to the conclusion that Qumran was most likely an Essene community.

Three centuries later some evidence turned up from nowhere that there actually was a group of Essenes in Jesus' time called the Nazarean Essenes. The Church Father Epiphanius, writing his Panarion, says there are seven different sects. He makes a clear distinction between two different groups: the Ossaeanes and the Nazareans. The Ossaeanes were Jews from lands beyond the Dead Sea who didn't believe in the books of Moses in the Hebrew Bible (Exodus, Deuteronomy, Numbers, Leviticus) and who encouraged celibacy. The Nazareans were Jews from the south where the early followers of Jesus are said to have fled after the martyrdom of Yuda, the brother of Jesus. Rather confusingly they acknowledged Moses and believed that he had received laws from God – but not the ones stated in the Hebrew Bible. They kept all the Jewish religious observances but did not offer sacrifices or eat meat. They encouraged marriage.

Both Josephus and Philo write about celibate Essenes having communal ownership and not involving themselves in trade. There's a strong implication that they only ate raw foods.

It's not really worth going into detail about the writings of the Dead Sea Scrolls which were discovered in the hills around Qumran, apart from outlining that they came in several distinct types of works: copies of the Hebrew Scriptures; commentaries on the Bible texts – with predictions about the last days and the Teacher of Righteousness; the Manual of Discipline with details of how to become a member of the community and live the Essene life; the War Scroll with a battle plan for the apocalypse; and the Copper Scroll which is just that. This scroll had to be cut into pieces to be read as it was too brittle to unroll. It appears to contain details of hidden treasure, but the Hebrew writing used has, so far, been uninterpretable because it has no religious content and the only ancient Hebrew that scholars understand comes from Biblical sources. We can almost certainly expect a *Da Vinci Code/Indiana Jones*-type movie based on the Copper Scroll before too long...

The general cut and thrust of all the Essenes was that they objected to the way Judaism was being run by the priests; rejected the Temple in Jerusalem as the centre of worship; turned away from animal sacrifice and thought they had the only valid path to the Truth. But it's very hard to tell whether the ones who lived in towns were of the same opinions as the ones who lived lives of separation in the desert, and which of them, exactly, were fine about marriage. There were graves of women found at Qumran but, just because a sect is celibate does not mean that it does not have women around somewhere. Opus Dei, the Catholic group that is featured (inaccurately) in *The Da Vinci Code*, is probably the most accurate modern example of Essene lifestyle. Opus Dei members can be celibates or married. The majority of the married ones live in their own homes in the world and the celibates live in Opus Dei centres. The married members are encouraged to have children (given the Catholic Church's ban on birth control) and the celibates are encouraged to live as separate a life as they can.

Given the fact that there's a group of Essenes called the Nazareans, this could be the answer to the appellation 'Jesus of Nazareth'. But there also is plenty of evidence against that supposition. It works nicely for the theory in this book that Jesus was married – because the Nazarean Essenes had no problem with marriage. However, Essenes didn't set foot in temples and this does cause a problem. Even though the best-known story about Jesus and the Temple in Jerusalem is when he turned over the money-changers' tables, this was because they were showing disrespect to the faith, not because he was disgusted by the Temple itself. Again, he grumbled about the Pharisees and the priests, but the gospels make it clear that he visited the Temple every day that he was in Jerusalem. In fact, Jesus asks his accusers before the crucifixion why they didn't take him when he was in the Temple: "I was daily with you in the temple, teaching."(Mark 3:49). Luke says pretty much the same (21:37): "And in the day time he was teaching in the temple; and at night he went out and abode in the mount that is called Olives. And all the people came early in the morning to him in the temple for to hear him."

Some people use this excerpt as evidence that Jesus lived with Mary and Martha in Bethany, which is located on the east slope of the Mount of Olives – and that this Mary was his wife Mary Magdalene but the evidence is very weak.

The third doubt about Jesus as an Essene is in his eating habits. We know already that he drank wine and we also know from the Last Supper that he took part in the Passover feast: "Then came the day of unleavened bread, when the Passover must be killed. And he sent Peter and John, saying, Go and prepare us the Passover, that we may eat." (Luke 22: 7). The Passover in this context means the Paschal lamb – the meat that is traditionally eaten for this most important of festivals. All meat that was eaten in Jesus' time *had* to be sacrificed to the Holy One whether at the Temple or by the local rabbi. To eat un-sacrificed meat was a blasphemy and eating sacrificed meat was a holy celebration. The mode of killing the animal sanctified it and the Jews believed that this was the most humane way possible of ending its life. The sacrifices ended when the Temple was destroyed in 70 CE, never to be built again to this day. Should it be rebuilt, the sacrifices would begin again.

The Passover was the culmination of this practice and the celebration of the liberation of the Israelites from years of slavery in Egypt. The lamb was central to the mythology and has remained so ever since. At the original Passover, lambs without blemish or mark were sacrificed and their blood smeared on the doorposts of the Israelites so that the Angel of

Death should know who they were and leave them alone when it came to kill all the firstborn of Egypt (Exodus 12:3-20). As this image of the sacrificial lamb represents Jesus in Christianity (and is mentioned no fewer than 25 times in the Book of Revelation, as well as with a clear connection in 1 Peter: "But with the precious blood of Christ, as of a lamb without blemish and without spot.") it would have been an anti-climax of the highest order for Jesus himself to have said "none for me thanks, I'm a vegetarian and I don't believe in sacrifice." There is a section in John that has been used to imply that Jesus hated the Temple and didn't eat meat, but careful reading of the extract shows no such thing; what he was protesting against was the defamation of the Temple by merchants who sold animals to people who hadn't been able to buy a bird or beast for sacrifice outside. He even calls the Temple "My Father's house" which is the strongest evidence yet that he wasn't a Temple-hating Essene.

"And the Jews' Passover was at hand, and Jesus went up to Jerusalem, and found in the temple those that sold oxen and sheep and doves, and the changers of money, sitting: And when he had made a scourge of small cords, he drove them all out of the temple, and the sheep, and the oxen; and poured out the changers' money, and overthrew the tables; And said unto them that sold doves, Take these things hence; make not my Father's house an house of merchandise." (John 2:13)

Many historians and theologians have tried to pull all this evidence together to make numerous conclusions. My favourite weaving together of all the information comes from Father Bargil Pixner, (1921–2002CE). He was a Benedictine monk of the Dormiton Abbey in Jerusalem, an archaeologist and author of *With Jesus Through Galilee According to the Fifth Gospel* (Corazin Publishing), in which he uses his knowledge of the seasons, flora and fauna and landscape of Galilee to demonstrate Jesus' movements and give background to his teaching. Father Pixner supports the idea (originated by the Early Church Father Jerome) that Jesus the Natzorean/Nazarene refers to his royal descent from King David. This follows on from the Isaiah 11:1 quotation: "A shoot will come up from the stump of Jesse and from his roots a branch will bear fruit." Jesse was the father of King David and branch is *netzer* in Hebrew. He also quotes the Talmud using Isaiah 14:19 "*You are thrown out, out of the grave like a despised shoot.*" (Tal Sanhedrin 43a). This uses the same Hebrew word for shoot. Father Pixner adds that the blind beggar, Bartimaeus, in Mark 10:47 and Luke 18:37 makes the link between Jesus and the royal line of Israel rather than the village. The crowd tells him that Jesus of Nazareth is coming (using the Greek phrase *ho Nazoraios* – the Natzorean) and Bartimaeus calls out "Jesus, son of David, have mercy on me!"

Father Pixner, being an archaeologist, has as valid a view on the status of the village of Nazareth as any. He says that it was an insignificant hamlet – and correctly states that it's never mentioned in the Hebrew Bible. He views it as a satellite of Japhia, a much larger town with its own military garrison, situated about a mile to the south-west – as opposed to Sepphoris which was four miles north-west.

The first known reference to Nazareth was discovered in 1962, on part of a marble plaque dating back to the third or fourth century CE. This plaque is in Hebrew rather than in Greek so it had the definitive spelling of Nazareth – and that spelling is the one that supports the idea of it meaning shoot or branch, and disassociates it clearly from the Nazarite ascetics who had a different root to the word. Father Pixner refers to the Qumran scrolls where the several hymns and psalms refer to the Essene community as "the Netzer shoot planted by God" (1QH vi 15, vii 5,8,10) and then makes a logical and feasible leap that the people of Nazareth were a small clan of descendents of David who returned from the Jewish exile in Babylon and settled together near a larger town and practiced their own brand of the Jewish faith.

He then adds the view that this clan was very influenced by Essene beliefs, if not totally a part of the Essenes. The evidence for this comes primarily from the fact that the Essenes used a Sun calendar, as we do, whereas the Jewish people then and now used a Moon calendar. Several times in the Bible, Father Pixner says Jesus appears to be working from a slightly different calendar from other people, notably when he says in John 8:1: "Go ye up unto this feast: I go not up yet unto this feast; for my time is not yet full come."

Being a Catholic monk, Father Pixner, quite understandably, is on the trail of Jesus' mother's perpetual virginity and he locates a parallel vow to the Nazarite one of separation in the Dead Sea Scrolls. He suggests that Mary had been vowed to a life of celibacy before her birth and was married to Joseph because he already had a family and would not require a wife who was willing to consummate the marriage.

If you look hard enough in the Bible – and in the Dead Sea Scrolls – you can find justification for pretty well any view that you want to take about any of the prophets, the women, the animals and the intentions of the writers. In the end it's only your own considered view, after taking all the evidence into consideration that counts. I can certainly take Father Pixner's findings on board; I find them feasible and, except for the Virgin Mary's part, likely. But even so, I can find no convincing evidence that Jesus was a long-term Nazarite or a fully-fledged celibate Essene. That lack of evidence makes him a common or garden Jew. And that, again, leaves the question of his marriage wide open.

CHAPTER FIVE

THE RIGHTS OF WOMEN, MARRIAGE
AND DIVORCE

The public Mikvah for both men and women had to be at a place of flowing water – and upstream of any place where washing or water-gathering was done, so that it was pure for the ritual cleansing that was so important to the Jewish faith. Nazareth's Mikvah was a full half-mile from the town, further than the well from where the women collected the water. Not for them the luxury of town-living with an aqueduct and private baths but there was, however, a white limestone building where the women could gather, have some privacy and discuss matters of importance amongst their own sex.

Judith and Tamar arrived at the Mikvah in Nazareth in the early afternoon, after a walk up and down hill that had tired Tamar's legs and left her toes blistered from the unaccustomed sandals. Both women's feet were white from the limestone dust on the path. For once, Judith had insisted on speed over comfort and had discouraged her daughter from stopping to admire the views to the North with its snow-capped mountains, or to the West where the blue Mediterranean could just be seen in the V of the hills. "Don't worry child," she said when Tamar complained. "Of all places, the Mikvah at Nazareth is the place where we can get salves to soothe your feet. And we can go home more slowly, I promise."

Judith's cousin, Miriam, was sitting outside the building together with a group of the other Nazarene women, including Leah's sister-in-law, Joanna, and the Rebbitzen, Sarah. Their children ran around them, playing, and once Tamar had washed her feet and greeted her relatives (who all exclaimed at how much she had grown), Judith sent her off to join the others. Although her daughter was nearly twelve she was still a child at heart.

"May I leave the sandals off?" said Tamar hopefully and grinned from ear to ear when her mother said "yes". Blisters were forgotten in the joy of bare feet again. Judith gathered up the discarded shoes and, after the regular family gossip was exchanged with her kin, asked to speak to Miriam, Joanna and Sarah in private.

"I wondered," said Miriam. "A visit at this time so often means a problem. I have time, Judith, and I'm sure Sarah does too."

"I have time," said Joanna, concern showing on her dark-skinned face.

The women sat, sharing some ripe figs, a little way from the building, and Judith told them about Leah, the likely divorce and the plans for Tamar. They discussed Leah first – the preservation of life was the greatest of the lesser commandments. The 613 rules given to Moses in the desert after the great 10 commandments could all be over-ruled in order to save a life.

"I am keeping her calm with poppy syrup so that her body has a chance to heal," said Judith, and the women nodded in assent. Opium was the best – and most dangerous – soporific of the time and it could also be used as a kind of anaesthetic both for mind and body. The sick could rest with a few sips of poppy syrup in a tea and the dying could be helped to depart in peace.

"Her mind I can do less about," Judith added. "I don't know if she would submit to having another wife over her. It may be divorce. And the only place she could come is here. But will her family have her?"

Joanna sat silently for a while and the others waited for her response first. "How likely is she to live?" she asked at last. "Is her heart broken?"

"Yes," said Judith simply. "I do not think she will live beyond six months."

"Not even for her daughters?"

"She does not understand how to value her daughters as they deserve to be valued."

Joanna flinched. *"I don't think my husband would accept her with any grace,"* she confessed. *"And I am not sure that I want her; there is enough to do and she was never easy."*

"We will manage, between us," said Sarah. *"If needs be she can stay in the room behind the Mikvah and help us there. We can always find room for a sister."*

The women looked at her gratefully; Sarah was a rock – sound and strong. Together with Miriam, the carpenter's wife, she all but ruled Nazareth, for everyone respected her good sense – and everyone knew that Miriam was a mystic. She could reach to the heart of a problem with a couple of words and often those who had gone to confess their fears and sins to her came away feeling healed in mind and body.

"I will make her a dose," said Miriam. *"Dandelion and hawthorn for her blood; olive leaf for her exhaustion; and eikon to protect her mind."* For a moment she was silent, musing on remedies. The other women waited respectfully.

"Susannah will help her," added Miriam at last. *"Judith, Susannah works at the Mikvah here for her keep. She is divorced so she will understand..."* she stopped, struck by an idea, but when the others questioned her, she put her hand up to show that she needed space to think. The women were silent, again; they knew their friend well. After a minute Miriam smiled and said, *"Yes, it could work. But we must hear the rest of the story first."* She nodded to Judith to continue.

Gratefully, Judith turned the subject to her daughter and the proposed marriage.

"If it's the will of the Lord, then I must submit," she said. *"But you and I, Miriam, have long spoken of Yeshua and Tamar becoming betrothed and I want my daughter to marry a boy that I believe she would suit well. She is fond of her uncle but she would find it so hard to adapt from niece to wife – and he's too old and too rough – and Leah, should*

she recover and decide to stay, would hate her; and rule her."

Instead of answering, Miriam burst into laughter.

"The answer is right in front of us," she said. "It is Susannah!"

"Yes, it could work," said Sarah, as both Judith and Joanna looked perplexed. "Susannah was the servant of my cousin Yohannes' first wife. He married Susannah to take care of his children when Rachel died. Susannah had her own son and, unfortunately, they both caught a brain fever. The boy died and she became deaf. Yohannes, who already has four sons from his first wife, decided that he did not want a deaf wife and divorced her."

"How cruel!" said Judith.

"Yes," said Miriam and Sarah together. "It was. But that is how things are."

"Susannah is twenty and beautiful," Sarah continued. "She has no family living. And she needs a new home in a new town – and a new husband."

"And there's more," said Miriam. "I don't suppose that your husband and brother-in-law have even told you that our boys - Yosef, Yuda and Yeshua - are working many days in Sepphoris now; they are all working on the new palace for Herod."

"No," said Judith, shaking her head. "Why haven't they come back to stay with us?"

"Probably because there is enough trouble in your house now as it is!" said Miriam dryly. "But if you would be willing to give them space so they would not have to travel back and forth so much then, in thanks, they could build you an extra room – always useful – and Susannah could go with them to help you women with the extra work."

"And?" said Judith.

"Susannah could take care of Leah. And Susannah would love to take care of Reuben. I know him, remember? He is a man who loves to be looked after – and Leah would never do that. Listen, I am not suggesting that you take her to Sepphoris to propose her as a wife for Reuben, but as *a helper for you. In the months it takes for Tamar to become menstrual, Reuben will have been so well cared for by Susannah that he might want her instead."*

"But would she want him?"

"She wants a home; security and kindness – and children," said Miriam. "Of course you can never know, but I think it is possible. It is worth trying."

The plan did work. Just as Miriam had predicted, Susannah's unusual fair beauty captivated Reuben – and Yacob too. And the lovely woman's deafness was not a problem; she could read lips and she was so grateful to be useful and appreciated that her willingness made up for the fact that she could appear a little slow. The men had been able to raise little argument to the idea of Yosef, Yuda and Yeshua staying in the house – Judith berated them over breaking the laws of hospitality and insisted (as was her right) on having her kinsmen under her roof. And it was Judith's responsibility to organise help in the house, so no one could complain about Susannah's new domestic role. She chafed a little at her own husband for looking too long at Susannah's lovely face but secretly she prayed that the plan might work.

Susannah had been frightened by the move at first. During the first few days, she was shy and clumsy, but then she confided her fears to Tamar, whose bed she shared. The two swiftly developed a bond, with Tamar helping Susannah when she did not understand and even developing a sign language that was easier for the older girl to grasp than half-seen words.

This was how Yeshua first saw Tamar, practising sign-language and laughing with Susannah. The older woman's beauty was familiar to him but Tamar's brightness and fun-filled smile were just what was needed to captivate the heart of an adolescent boy. Before long, both he and Yuda were teasing her whenever they met and Tamar was blushing every time that they spoke to her. She began to carry their breakfast to the synagogue every morning, with her father and brother's food, and she loved to walk alongside Yeshua to the workshop where they ate. His long limbs could outpace her easily, so every third step she would add a skip that made him laugh. After a week he was carrying her basket for her.

When Reuben spoke to Leah about his plans either to divorce her or to find a second wife, the anger that exploded from her heart saved her life. Leah's will reasserted itself and she refused to die. Judith wondered how much of her recovery was due to Miriam's herbs which Leah had at first refused but then been given almost forcibly. "You are in my care; you eat my food; you will take my medicine," said Judith. Leah obeyed.

She berated Reuben loudly both alone and in front of witnesses – this was sufficient to offer grounds for divorce alone, as Judith told her gently. She would not be well enough to travel to Nazareth for four full months but she made it clear from the start that she chose divorce over polygamy.

"I will not be a second wife," she spat at her husband.

"You would come first," he said placatingly, knowing he was lying. He would never take her to his bed again and the wife who was bedded was the first wife, no matter how senior her predecessor. Leah turned her back on him from then on and, changing tactics abruptly, never spoke to him again. She accepted Susannah's quiet ministrations to her tired and aching body but mocked her deafness behind her back. Leah was all bitterness and Judith did not have enough knowledge of herbs to try to help once Miriam's brew was finished. At least, as Judith said later, by the Lord's grace, Reuben never mentioned Tamar's name to Leah as the second wife he hoped to take.

Yosef took Leah back to Nazareth on the back of his donkey as soon as she was well enough. Leah said goodbye to her daughters coolly and, although they wept that their mother was going, they held tightly to Susannah, already an affectionate substitute for an embittered mother who could not love her daughters because they were girls.

"We will go and see Mother every weekend," promised Susannah. But everyone knew that the frequency would drop until the estrangement was complete.

It was a relief to everyone once Leah had left, but Judith, who had been her friend and confidante, missed the company of another woman her own age. She was glad to hear from Susannah's visits with the children that Leah struck lucky. She married an elderly widower whose first wife had been a nag and whose children had grown up and left Nazareth. He just wanted company. Susannah told Judith and Tamar as they wove together, speaking in the soft monotone that she had developed after losing her hearing: "She makes his life a misery but that's just what his first wife did and he's used to that. And she's fiercely proud of him to outsiders. She makes sure he's the best-dressed and fed man in the town. So all are content in their way."

The dress that they were weaving was Susannah's wedding dress. Her gentleness with Reuben's children had won his respect as much as her beauty pleased his eye. He cavilled for a while because of her deafness but, for some reason – and no one but Tamar noticed how it happened – Susannah had begun to hear again.

"It was you," said Tamar quietly to Yeshua beside the fire one evening. "You went outside with her and put your hands over her ears. And the next day, when I dropped the copper bowl, she turned round at the noise." Yeshua just grinned at her and put his finger to his lips. Tamar felt a warm flush run through her at the idea that he was somehow special – and that they shared a secret.

Marriage rules

The Talmud taught that a man should first study Torah and then marry so, as Sepphoris was already becoming well known as a centre for study, if Yeshua were living and working in Sepphoris he could easily have studied with the wise men who lived there. The sages taught that the perfect age for a man to marry was 18, if he were to be trusted to keep his thoughts pure until then, but the rabbis were very aware of the dangers of sexual fantasy – and of premarital sex. Rabbi Huna is reported in Talmud as saying that a man not married by the age of 20 would spend all his days in sinful thoughts (Kiddushin 29b) – and Rabbi Hisda claimed to be superior to other rabbis because he had married at 16. He added he would have been even better if he had married at 14, because he would have been completely free of impure thoughts (Kiddushin 29b-30a).

Even though Talmud wasn't written down until after Jesus' time, it is known that it reported the views on marriage of the previous generation. The High Priest of Israel was required to marry a girl within six months after she reached puberty. Marriage was contracted in two stages: *erusin* and *nissu'in*. The *erusin* was a betrothal (which we would call an engagement), a ceremony where the potential bridegroom declared "Be thou consecrated unto me ..." before two eligible witnesses, such as the girl's parents. Talmud says (Kid. 2b) this is "a setting aside of the woman like a consecrated object" prohibited to the rest of the world and it was regarded as a legal contract. However, Talmud says that she is not "permitted to him" despite Deuteronomy 20:7 which strongly implies the opposite: "And what man is there that hath betrothed a wife, and hath not taken her? Let him go and return unto his house, lest he die in the battle, and another man take her."

If either of the betrothed couple died before the wedding, they inherited nothing from each other and any act of infidelity on the woman's part was treated as adultery. The penalty for all adultery was to be stoned to death. That was why it was so very important that Joseph was willing to marry the Virgin Mary when she fell pregnant. She would not have lived to carry an illegitimate child to term.

The rabbis in Jesus' day laid down the law that the maximum period of time allowed for a betrothal to last was a year. This was to prevent men from changing their minds or keeping the woman dangling with no further commitment. It was enforced by the fact that if a man waited more than a year, he was legally required to support his bride financially, whether or not he married her. The rabbis thought that another problem with a long engagement was temptation and this fear obviously became much more of an issue in later centuries – by the twelfth century couples were encouraged to become betrothed in the morning, get married in the afternoon and consummate the marriage before sunset.

Every single aspect of marriage is covered in Talmud – with seven sections of the women's section (Nashim). They are:

Yevamot (Levirates; *i.e.* husband's brothers),
Ketubbot (Marriage Contracts),
Nedarim (Vows),
Nazir (the Nazarite vow of celibacy),
Sota (A Woman Suspected of Adultery),
Gittin (Divorce),
Qiddushin (Marriage ceremony).

Both the Palestinian and Babylonian Talmuds have Gemara (critical commentaries) on each of the seven sections. It's worth looking at these commentaries.

Responsibilities

If a woman is widowed, especially if she has no child, one of her husband's brothers is expected to marry the widow in order to support her and give her children. When brothers live together, and one of them dies childless, the dead man's wife shall not be allowed to marry an outsider. Her husband's brother must cohabit with her, making her his wife, and thus performing a brother-in-law's duty to her. The first-born son whom she bears will then perpetuate the name of the dead brother, so that his name will not be obliterated from Israel (Deuteronomy 25:5-6). There was a strange way of getting out of this commandment, a rather less hostile version of which can be found in the Biblical Book of Ruth:

"The elders of his city shall summon him and speak to him. If he remains firm, he must say, 'I do not want to take her.' His sister-in-law shall then approach him before the elders, take off his shoe and spit toward his face. She shall then declare, 'This is what shall be done to the man who will not build up a family for his brother.'" (Deuteronomy 25:7-10)

In Ruth's case it wasn't quite pertinent because her suitor, Boaz, was a cousin of her mother-in-law rather than brother of her late husband, but the principle remains; Boaz went to the man closer to her in kin and asked him to let go of his right to marry Ruth by taking off his shoe. It all goes to show that marriage and having children to beget heirs was thought of as vitally important.

Perhaps unsurprisingly this commandment is not kept today although, should the occasion arise, a *Beth Din* or council of ten Jewish elders still meets to absolve the dead man's brother from keeping it. That the commandment was kept in Jesus' time is evidence of a sort that he did not have a wife living when he was crucified. Had he been married to Mary Magdalene his brother, Yuda, as the eldest brother, would have been obligated to marry her and have children with her. This would have been the case, even if Yuda were a half-brother as the Church has often taught.

Marriage contract

The second commandment, *Ketubbot,* refers to the *Ketubah,* or marriage contract, where the husband states that he will provide food, clothing and companionship for his wife, and that he will pay a pre-agreed sum of money if he divorces her. This is a kind of pre-nuptual contract although the money allowed was generally only sufficient for her to be able to support herself for one year. If he died and left her as a widow, she could collect the *Ketubah* money from his estate. She also reinherited any property that she brought into the marriage. Most of the contracts after the second century also included details of the Talmudic requirements of marriage including sexual duties.

Jewish marriage contracts were written down by a scribe and many of them are breathtakingly beautiful especially medieval ones with illuminations such as you see in ancient bibles. They would be hung in the married couple's home both as objects of beauty and as reminders of the couple's obligations to each other. In Jesus' day the contract included details of the wife's dowry. This had to be provided by her father; a second daughter was entitled to a dowry as large as her elder sister's and if that wasn't possible, she could claim ownership of a tenth of all her father's immovable property – rather like a mortgage. It's no wonder then that daughters were seen as a mixed blessing.

When a girl's father died, his sons were required to maintain their sisters and endow each of them with a tenth of what they had inherited. This was law even if there were ten sisters and it meant the men were left with nothing.

A dowry could be made up from money, jewellery, property or whatever both families considered to be of value. The husband had to add an extra fifty per cent of what the wife's family gave and the wife was entitled to a tenth of the total to use for her own expenses. When there was no dowry available at all, the husband-to-be was expected to give his betrothed at least enough for her to buy herself a wedding outfit. And it was stipulated that this money should be given to her *before* the wedding!

Other parts of the contract stated that a husband could not oblige his wife to leave the country if he decided to move; nor to change a town for a country residence or vice versa. And she had a right to be housed in the kind of dwelling – or better – than that in which they started their marriage. Every contract was slightly different and was thrashed out at the time of the betrothal.

Nowadays a *Ketubah* is still required for an orthodox Jewish marriage and it must be signed by two witnesses in the same way as a register must be signed in all legal marriages today.

In Jesus' time, the betrothal was made legally valid by the man giving his wife a gift of money or by a letter of betrothal. Some people dispensed with the formalities even then and simply moved in together, but this was viewed with great disapproval by rabbis and the religiously-minded, even though a marriage was much more a legal matter than a religious one.

The wedding

Before the wedding ceremony, or *Qiddushin*, the bride had to visit the Mikvah, for purification. Nowadays, ultra-orthodox Jewish brides are required to produce a certificate proving that they have attended a Mikvah. The ceremony itself was simple and to the point. The bride was led into the house of the bridegroom and a few basic formalities were carried out. These varied by location and local custom: for example, in Judea there were always two groomsmen (like best men), one each for the bride and the groom. It was their job to smooth over any problems in negotiations and on the day itself. However, in Galilee there was no such practice.

The vows, or *Nedarim*, varied according to the time and place, but a whole section on all sorts of vows made by Jewish people are included in the marriage section of Talmud because of the last two sections, which refer to the fact that a woman's father and her husband have the power to annul any vows that she has made (making vows was disapproved of by rabbis at that time – they were generally vows of abstinence). The importance of this is that, should the Virgin Mary have made a Nazarite vow, Yosef would have had the power to annul it on the day they got married.

As might be expected, the rules and regulations around the day of a Jewish wedding were fairly complicated. Nobody got married at a festival time in case the celebrations got confused or the Sabbath rest was threatened. A maiden got married on Wednesday afternoons which allowed her husband to make a formal complaint to the court of Sanhedrin – who sat every Thursday – if he found on the wedding night that he'd been taken for a sucker as to his bride's virtue. Widows married on a Thursday as no similar valid complaint could be made against them!

The bride had a wedding veil – her face and hair had to be covered for the actual ceremony – and there was either a veil spread over the couple or a tent built for the wedding to take place in. Nowadays this is known as a *chupah* – a canopy on four poles under which a marriage takes place. The *chupah* covering can sometimes be the man's *talit* or prayer shawl. In very ancient days and perhaps still in Jesus' time the couples wore crowns, as still pertains in Greek Orthodox weddings. Palm and myrtle branches were carried in front of them and grain or money thrown as confetti. Music preceded the procession which all who met were expected to join – as a religious duty. Girls carrying lamps on sticks like torches (the wise and foolish virgins of Matthew 25:1) guided the bridegroom to his bride and the celebrations stretched to a full week of festivities. The bride and groom were expected to keep to themselves during that week having as much sex as possible – hence the passage in Genesis when Jacob has been fooled into marrying Leah instead of his beloved Rachel and the girls' father tells him to "fulfil her week" (Genesis 29:27) before he will give Jacob Rachel as a bride too.

Divorce
Gittin are the rules for divorce. Grounds for divorce included any interpretation of "uncleanliness" which included every kind of breach of propriety from not observing the ritual laws of cleansing to shouting at your husband so that the neighbours could overhear. Spinning thread in the street, going around with your hair un-plaited, or being rude to your parents were other offenses. A universal get-out clause in fact! Divorcing someone because they became deaf was quite feasible; anything that gave one partner a disgust for the other was valid. And a woman could *make* a man divorce her either because he was repulsive to her or if he refused to have sex with her.

Simple divorce meant the husband handing the wife a letter of divorcement in front of two witnesses. But there was also the matter of a religious divorce, called a *get*. This was vital for a woman to be able to marry again and, even nowadays, bitter battles are fought between Jewish divorced couples where an ex-husband refuses to grant the *get*.

A woman might not marry a third time whether or not she had a *get*. It's interesting that *Nazir* (the Nazarite vow of celibacy) is placed in the Talmudic section on marriage laws but is reflected in the Book of Numbers among the laws for women – rules of separation were very important within a marriage and it was possible, and even likely, that a couple could make a mutual Nazarite vow during the time of the woman's menses and end it at the time she was permitted to return. The time stated was from the first issue of blood through to seven full days after the last bleeding. This practice of separation is still observed today by orthodox Jewry and, despite modern views of the idea being barbaric, many orthodox Jews say that it keeps marriages passionate and strong to have a regular time of abstinence.

Sota deals with the penalties for an adulteress – or a suspected adulteress. Numbers 5:15 rules that if a jealous husband accuses his wife of adultery, she must either accept divorce or attempt to prove her innocence by going with him to a priest. She is then required to drink a brew into which the name of God (generally forbidden to be spoken or written) has been dissolved. These "bitter waters" will kill her if she is unfaithful – and also kill her lover too. If she is innocent, no harm will come to her (Numbers 5:22-28).

This sounds savage but the woman could refuse to drink the bitter waters on any grounds she liked including those that she couldn't live with such a suspicious husband. A woman who did not mind divorce or losing her *ketubah* – her marriage settlement – did not have a problem. But of course, most women minded very much.

The Spanish Jewish philosopher and Kabbalistic mystic Nachmanides wrote that, of all the 613 commandments, only the *sota* law required God's actual co-operation to work as the bitter waters could only be effective miraculously. The Torah claims that guilty adulterers will suffer horrible deaths on drinking the bitter waters. It also promises innocent women who are wrongfully accused, but who elect to go through the humiliating *sota* experience to demonstrate their innocence, will conceive a child even if they were previously barren.

The law for proven adulterers of either sex is in Leviticus 20. The law is death – as it is for homosexuality, bestiality and for sleeping with a mother and her daughter, whether or not the man is related to them.

Law and sex

Just to finish, Hebrew scripture and rabbinic tradition are unique among all ancient law codes, in actually laying down the law on how often a husband must make love to his wife.

Ketuboth (62a) sets out a timetable based on the man's profession so that he can fulfil his obligation as a husband and still perform his duties at work. A man who was independently wealthy and didn't have to work was expected to make love to his wife (should she want him to) every night; a camel driver on the other hand was only expected to perform sexually once a month – and a sailor only twice a year.

Someone "dedicated to Torah and Talmud study" was required to have sex with his wife once a week, preferably on Friday night. Scholars of the law were warned against acting like roosters in having too much sex (Berachot 22a), but even a scholar was responsible for maximizing his wife's pleasure when he did make love to her. And if it were the night that she had just returned from the Mikvah, after purifying herself from her menses, *all* husbands, regardless of occupation, had a sacred duty to have sex with their wives. The cynical could say that this was mostly because it was the most likely time for her to conceive but it certainly ensured that husband and wife were reunited in a way that was intended to promote intimacy between them.

CHAPTER SIX

ORIGINAL SIN AND THE DIVINE FEMININE

Yeshua and Tamar were betrothed at the Festival of Tabernacles and married in the month before Passover the following year. Yeshua by then was seventeen and Tamar fourteen. The wrangles that accompanied their betrothal were no different from the many other families around them – how much money for the dowry; how much of that should be matched by the husband? The most contentious issue was where they should live.

The wife moved into the husband's house; it was traditional. But Yeshua, his brother Yuda, and father Yosef, worked so often in Sepphoris – and had even built their own room onto the house – that it was decided that they should spend most of their time there. Tamar would be married in Yeshua's family home in Nazareth and, when she was not pregnant, would travel with her husband to Nazareth once a month for the Sabbath Eve. Both mothers were happy with this plan for they got to see their children regularly and the distance was short for young legs.

The wedding feast went on for seven full days as was customary. None of it was strange to Tamar as she had been to so many other weddings of family and friends. But it was strangely un-nerving to be the bride; the one receiving gifts and the one to receive all the prayers and good wishes from the women for a quick conception and easy pregnancies and birth. As was customary, the marriage was expected to be consummated immediately after the wedding, so that any imperfections in Tamar's virtue could be known and responded to. Not that this often happened with a couple as young as they, but it was still a little un-nerving to be shut into a room with her new husband while people outside sang and danced with the occasional cat-call from the young men, knowing exactly what would be going on.

Of course Tamar was no stranger to the facts of the marital bed; her home had little privacy and Judith had talked carefully with her before her betrothal about all that she would experience. Judith, as a good mother and a happy wife, made a good advisor for her daughter and there was no unnecessary fear.

As it was, Yeshua surprised her by breaking with the custom. Instead of a rather rushed and nervous coupling, they spent the time giggling after he whispered to her that he thought they should wait until they had a little more time and privacy, and just let the others think that they had lain together. This little deception did more to make them friends than anything else and that first time spent totally alone, cuddling without any pressure, helped them both to feel pleasant anticipation for the future. Yeshua even pricked his finger with his knife to make a tiny stain on the blanket and the naughtiness of the deception and the secret that they shared showed in their eyes throughout the rest of the celebrations. Judith and Miriam relaxed, knowing all was well and that their children had every chance of being happy together.

The wedding was closely followed by Tamar's first ever visit to Jerusalem. Passover – or Pesach – was one of the most important of the five Jewish festivals and all orthodox men travelled to the great city to celebrate it. Women, when they could, went too, although the pregnant, sick or those with newborns were expected to stay at home.

For Tamar, with the new status of marriage, new clothes and an attentive husband who made her laugh and held her hand whenever others could not see, the journey was an adventure and a delight. Both Tamar's and Yeshua's family made the journey this time and it was the first journey where Tamar regretted the segregation of men and women at the boarding houses along the way. She missed her husband's company and it showed in a sulky face that made the other women laugh.

"That won't last!" said several of the other women with the hindsight of experience. Dinah's voice loudest of all. Tamar's sister was jealous of

her obvious happiness; her own fondness for her husband had faded rapidly.

"But it's good that it's there at all," said Judith, defending her daughter fondly. "Let her be."

Jerusalem was a revelation; an enormous walled city filled with bustle, merchants, stalls, scents, color and comment. It seemed as though the whole place rang with gossip. Most of the marriage arrangements between families were made at the festival times and, with the bustle of visits to the Temple, purchases and visits to distant family members, the time passed in a blur. Tamar was aghast by the size of the Temple; she had never imagined a building so big. Just climbing the steps to the Mikvah took her higher than she had ever stood and her head swam when she looked out across rooftops.

Some local people laughed at the little provincial with her wide, scared eyes as she refused to believe that she could see over the city walls to the open land beyond. Her eyes must be deceiving her! The hilly landscape at home was one thing but to be elevated so high on a building was completely disorientating. As was the Mikvah itself. Room after room for washing and cleansing; bustling attendants handing out drying cloths; women going through the bath ritual at what seemed like lightning speed to keep the queue from spreading out into the street. Although Tamar had experienced the Mikvah in Sepphoris, she only went at the regulated time after the end of her menstruation and then with her mother. This time, in the crowds of women, she was separated from Judith and Dinah and found herself almost roughly pushed into the water – surprisingly cold – and the unexpectedness of it made her cough and choke.

In the Temple itself, she gazed wide-eyed around the vast court of the Gentiles while the men-folk changed their local money for the Temple tithe and the group was approached by a series of orange, fig, date and nut-sellers offering their wares. It was a marketplace all of its own with people hustling and bustling, children crying and screaming and the scent of the dung of the animals being taken for sacrifice mingling with the strange, acrid smoke that blew across from the sacrificial area. Tamar stayed with the women in the Court of the Women while their menfolk took the animals and birds through to the Court of the Men and the priests. The thought of animal sacrifice did not worry her. She had never been raised with anthropomorphic views about animals; meat was always a treat and she had been trained from the very beginning that this was their purpose: to be sacrificed to the Lord before being eaten.

Even so, as the festival of Passover continued and the family visited the Temple every day, she was glad to be with Yeshua. His religious knowledge was tempered with good sense and kindness and every word gave evidence of his light heart. Not for him the ultra-serious theoretical debates that went on night and day in the Temple with the men arguing, shouting and debating a point of law with angry faces. Tamar did not have to spend endless hours in the Court of the Women while her husband sat at the feet of sages, or queued to be able to make an important religious point that most of the people in the Court of the Men totally ignored. When he did leave her there, from what she could see from the balcony over-looking the men's part of the Temple, Yeshua drew his own crowds; he did not have to wait and see anyone. She felt her heart swell with pride for him when she realised how popular he was. Someone actually walked past her saying "that young man is a prophet," and she treasured the words.

Miriam had told her of a time when Yeshua, at the age of twelve, had got lost on the way home from the Temple. "At least, we thought he was lost," said Miriam wryly. "He was as happy as a free-flying bird in the Court of the Men, asking questions that most of the priests could not answer – and giving his own answers back."

"Were they angry with him?" she asked.

"Some of them were," said Miriam. "They said he must be quoting from some sage whose words he had committed to rote; but others were impressed. He is very wise."

She looked at Tamar. "Does his faith worry you?" she asked gently.

"Sometimes," Tamar admitted. "It's so strong; so...so...real. I can't quite understand it. He talks of the letter of the law and the spirit of the law but I don't understand the difference."

"Hmmm," said Miriam. "Often the difference is kindness." That Tamar could understand. She nodded her head, smiling. "Oh yes," she said. "He is always kind. Even when he is stern with people he is not angry. Have you noticed?"

Miriam laughed. "He does get angry!" she said. "But I do know what you mean. He never looks at people as if they were deliberately doing him wrong; he always sees why they are as they are."

That was a little too difficult for a young wife to understand, but she held on to the glow of being a holy man's wife. It helped her to cope with the strange feelings of longing that she had begun to experience when he was not around and the frustrations of always being with the other women, preparing food, sitting apart at the tables, looking after the children instead of sitting next to Yeshua and laughing with him over supper as they did at home.

Back in Sepphoris, it was easier at first. Tamar's happiness was visible as she continued with her old life but with the addition of a husband. But that could not last for long. So easily, she slipped back into old habits; spending time chatting to friends at the market; helping Susannah with her latest baby and assuming that nothing more was needed of her. When the first signs of her menstruation came she was disappointed not to be pregnant but horrified that she should now sleep separately from her husband and move to the women's side of the house for a whole 14 days. No touch of the hand; no hugs or cuddles – she couldn't bear it! Always before, the ritual of separation had been a happy time where the women gave themselves little treats such as honey cakes or telling stories. This time, Tamar lied to herself, to Yeshua and to her mother and pretended that she was still clear for just one extra, precious night. In the morning, Yeshua noticed. He said nothing to her but there was a kind of hurt in his eyes that Tamar did not react to; she was sure it was disappointment, just like hers. It did not occur to her that her desires had made him ritually impure and meant that he must visit the Mikvah that evening before being able to go again to synagogue. He was in the middle of some complicated study there that Tamar did not understand and was not interested in – but which required his presence every day. That day, he would not be able to go.

"Tamar, you must tell me next time," he said, gently.

"I didn't know," she lied, swiftly. It was so easy.

"Are you not guided by the moon's times?" he said, believing her and assuming that her times were irregular.

"Not always," she said. Another lie.

Guilt did touch her that day and, to make up for her fib, she laid out a new woven robe that she had been working on for him that he could wear and think of her while they could not be together. She tidied up their little room, with its precious curtain that gave them some privacy and laid a fresh blanket for him to sleep on.

Instead of joining in with the women's time cheerfully, she was withdrawn and sulky. Susannah and Judith misunderstood the reason for this and tried to comfort her. "It's very early days," they said. "It can take months to conceive. Enjoy your time of freedom!"

When Yeshua came back from work that night, he smiled at his young wife and gave her a "yes, I miss you too" kind of look. But he did not put on the new robe and, at the end of that evening, he did not sleep in their bed but where Reuben and Jacob were sleeping. That hurt Tamar's feelings. If she had thought, she would have realised that everything she had touched for the last day and night was ritually impure and that, had he worn her robe and slept in her bed, he would not be able to go and study for a second day.

The other women noticed too and thought it a little strange but none of them thought to doubt Tamar's word on when her time of withdrawal had come. Anger burnt in her stomach at the injustice of life and she went back to her own bed to sleep instead of sleeping with Judith and Susannah so missing out on feminine comfort and the happy stories they told. Without her, they were less happy too.

On the evening of the second day, Yeshua changed the bedding in the little room and took the new robe with him to the Mikvah where, the law said, he must go again for touching anything that a menstrual woman had touched. He said not a word of reproach to his wife; why would he? She had made a genuine mistake. For just one moment, the following morning, his face showed a flicker of impatience when Tamar forgot again and ran up to take his hand to tell him that the youngest she-goat had had a kid. He pulled his hand away just before she could touch it and the shock of rejection made her stop dead, blood draining from her face.

"Tamar..." he said gently, but she turned away, her shoulders shaking as a lump rose in her throat. "Tamar..." and, because he loved her and her happiness was so important to him, he caught hold of her by the shoulders to turn her and pull her into his arms. What matter for another day away from the synagogue? What matter for another ritual bath; his little wife was important to him. But he was just too late. The tightness of his hands on her shoulders implied reproach to a girl who was already filled with resentment and guilt. She wriggled away and ran back into the house.

Tamar nursed the little lovers' quarrel; she could not let it go because to confess her original deception would have made her wrong. She was just religious enough to fear the Lord over the breaking of what now seemed to her to be a very silly law, but she was quite young enough to think that her husband would disregard it too if he really loved her. That Yeshua had willingly made himself impure by trying to catch her and tell her that he was sorry after having missed his studies twice and needing to go for yet another ritual bath made it worse. He was good and she was bad. She was very young, helplessly in love and very confused.

It was easy after that to start resenting Yeshua's time at the synagogue and resenting having to travel to Nazareth once a month. On the surface there seemed to be nothing wrong between them that was not wrong with a hundred other Jewish couples in Galilee, but the small currents of discontent that form early can have long-term effects.

In the third month, Tamar refused to travel to Nazareth with her husband. She said the journey was preventing her from getting pregnant. Looking at the stubborn face before him, Yeshua sighed. Of course, she wanted him to stay behind with her but he would not.

"My family are as important to me as yours are to you," he said.

"But I should be more important than they are!" she said petulantly.

"You are," he said. "Which is why I spend three and a half weeks every month with you here. It is your wish to live with your family that is the only thing that keeps us here. There is work for me in towns other than Sepphoris."

She construed this as a dislike of her family and when he went to Nazareth without her, she had a tantrum of such violence that she was almost hysterical. She saw his silence and his refusal to quarrel with her as weakness.

The following month, Tamar was still not pregnant. This time she blamed it on her husband who had not lain with her so often. She carried the burden of resentment deep inside and was shrewish with him, trying to push and provoke him into some kind of reaction so she could cry and offer blame.

When the time came to go to Nazareth again, she once more refused, but this time he insisted. He invoked the help of her parents and Susannah who, between them, got her red-faced and sullen onto the back of a donkey, and sent her off regardless of her misery.

"Miriam will sort it," said Judith hopefully. She had seen her daughter's increasing unhappiness.

"But will she listen to his mother when it is him she is so angry with?" said Susannah.

"It's not him; it's herself," said Judith with the wisdom of years. "And I do hope so."

Common courtesy made Tamar behave prettily when she and Yeshua *reached Nazareth, but her withdrawal from her husband was very obvious and the atmosphere that evening was strained. After supper, Miriam invited Tamar onto the roof of the little house for a chat. Her daughter-in-law resisted but Miriam's look of kindness won through and, eventually, she gave in. As they sat on the rush mats and looked up at the stars above, enjoying the coolness of the breeze, Miriam said: "What was the very first thing that went wrong?"*

Taken by surprise, Tamar gaped at her.

"The very first," said Miriam. "The very first mistake; the very first tiny deception; the first loss of faith."

"It wasn't me," said Tamar.

"It's always you," said Miriam. "It's always me. It's always him. It's always every one of us. Later I will ask Yeshua exactly the same question. It doesn't matter which of you was first in making a mistake, the truth is that each of you made a first mistake. Will you tell me yours?"

Tamar told her the truth. It was like a boil being lanced. Miriam helped her to see that it wasn't the breaking of the law itself that had hurt her but her reaction to it; her blame and her fear of being found out. Then they discussed the law and why it was followed; the importance of discipline in word and thought and deed. Not discipline imposed by others but self-discipline to build reserves of inner strength.

Later, Miriam spoke to Yeshua and, when the young couple went to bed they talked it through, both nervous and not knowing how the other would feel. But the talking healed the wounds and they held each other tightly, realising how close they had come to living a marriage blighted by one, simple disobedience of a law that didn't make sense to a young couple in love. From then on, there was a new peace and understanding between them.

In the years to come, by mutual agreement, they sometimes relaxed their observance of some of the laws, but it was always by discussion and accord and never again by deceit. As Yeshua said, the spirit of the law was more important than the letter of the law and they should not make

the mistake of allowing the law to be more important than their marriage.
Breaking with tradition, they built themselves a little home of their own,
still connected to Tamar's family but with its own front door, so that she
could be mistress of her own home and he could be master. They built a
life together that was uniquely theirs and together they discovered that
loving kindness practised with discipline was greater than any other law.

Purity

Tamar's one little deceit could have become the breeding ground for a
hundred other points of discord – as many other men and women have
discovered to their cost. Of course, it is not only women who sow the first
seed of discontent but, ever since the creation of Eve, it is women who
usually receive the blame for it. And that is from other women as well as
from men. For as long as Judaism, Islam and Christianity have been
mainstream religions, they have faced long and unproductive battles over
the idea of Original Sin and the concept of the feminine as inferior and,
in same cases, even evil.

The Jewish laws of purity were just as fierce for men as they were for
women, but they were – and are – more visible in a sex which bleeds as
a part of its menstrual cycle. All bloodshed renders an orthodox Jew
impure, whether it is a natural process, a thorn in a finger or a wound
sustained in battle. However, there is no doubt that women, down the
ages, have got the majority of the blame for all of humanity's problems.
If Eve could only have obeyed, then we would all be fine – wouldn't we?

I think not. The problem stems more from Adam being tempted by
Eve, and that is the root of the fear of the feminine that runs throughout
religious teaching. In the Old Testament, we can read the stories of many
"bad" women: Eve who ate of the Tree of Knowledge of Good and Evil;
Rebekah who deceived her husband; Delilah who un-manned Samson;
and the notorious Jezebel, murderess, harlot and perpetrator of fraud. But
the Old Testament also offers us Cain, who kills his brother; Saul who is
jealous, moody and disobedient; David, who sends a man to his death so

he can marry his wife; and Solomon who is a letch and an idolater. Nevertheless, the fact that Eve is portrayed as causing the fall of humanity takes some living down.

However, we do have a choice: we can take on board the commentaries by male-only experts who were living in a time where social and sexual customs were different from our own – or we can read the teachings ourselves and make up our own minds. All through this book it has been important to remember who wrote the commentary – when, where, why and for what audience. The Bible and all religious teachings provide us with exactly what we are looking for, whether it is evidence of strength or weakness, clarity or convention. Where we are prejudiced, we will find evidence to support that prejudice.

Original and deeper teachings can be found than those which are presented on the surface. Most of these, read from the metaphysical viewpoint rather than as straight story-telling, relate to masculine and feminine aspects within each human, but are presented to refer to men and to women rather than to the complexities within each one of us. If the Bible is read as a psychological, spiritual, mystical and metaphysical story it becomes much clearer – the whole story of the development of human understanding is there, with mistakes made and learnt from, over generations of lives. In the women's case in particular, the stories progress significantly in self-awareness and inner development, from the Matriarchs who make every mistake in the book through to Ruth who leaves the tribe to create her own life, and Deborah, the Judge of all Israel.

The total feminine according to Kabbalistic teaching is: darkness, death, the word "no", contraction, discipline, judgement/discernment, night, negativity, receptivity, passivity, softness. The total masculine according to Kabbalistic teaching is: light, birth, the word "yes", expansion, mercy, day, positivity, activity, hardness, strength.

Strategy is feminine; tactics are masculine. Listening is feminine; talking is masculine. Eating is feminine; cooking is masculine. Singing is masculine; listening to music is feminine. So, you can see that we all contain both traits. The masculine gives; the feminine receives.

Often, women hate this idea, thinking it implies weakness and an unwritten law that women shouldn't be powerful. But even a moment's thought shows that an over-balance on giving or expanding is as lethal as over-contracting. Cancer in the body is the continual over-expansion of cells. A good life is one which balances giving and receiving. It is nature that man gives the seed for conception and woman receives it. But then woman gives the food and nourishment to the growing foetus which, in turn receives it. That is how the balance of male and female works.

It is sometimes hard for women to accept this even though the later stories of women in the Bible show how use of the feminine as strength is incredibly powerful.

Lilith

There is also one ancient part-Biblical legend which is used as an even bigger sword with which to beat women than the story of Eve. This is the story of Lilith: a powerful legend which appears at first sight to show that women who will not take orders from men and accept second place to them are demons. Lilith was Adam's first wife. She appears only in the oral tradition with the back-up evidence for her existence taken from Genesis 1:37:

> "So God created man in his image, in the image of God created he him; male and female created he them. And God blessed them, and God said unto them, Be fruitful, and multiply, and replenish the earth, and subdue it: and have dominion over the fish of the sea, and over the fowl of the air, and over every living thing that moveth upon the earth."

All well and good; most people would take that to mean Eve. However, in Genesis 2:18 it then says: "And the Lord God said, 'It is not good that the man should be alone; I will make a helper for him.'" Eve was then created from Adam's rib (a better translation is "from one side" i.e. one half). But, if God had already created two beings, male and female, what had happened to the first female?

The stories which have come down through Jewish folklore and the Kabbalistic tradition state that the first woman was Lilith – Adam's equal. Lilith refused to be Adam's wife and ran away and Eve was created from Adam's side to replace her. If it is Eve who is blamed for the fall from the Garden of Eden by not obeying the rules, it is Lilith who is blamed if any woman becomes uppity and wants to take over the place of a man. There is one reference naming Lilith in the Bible: "The wild beasts of the desert shall also meet with the wild beasts of the island, and the satyr shall cry to his fellow; Lilith also shall rest there, and find for herself a place of rest." (Isaiah 34:7). However, the King James Bible for some unknown reason translates the Hebrew for Lilith as "screech owl" so this reference is mostly overlooked.

She is also mentioned in the Dead Sea Scrolls: "The spirits of the destroying angels, spirits of the bastards, demons, Lilith, howlers, and … those which fall upon men without warning to lead them astray from a spirit of understanding," (Song for a Sage 4Q510-511). She is also mentioned (although not by name) in the sixth century Jewish commentary Midrash Rabbah and in the seminal Kabbalistic work *The Zohar* (Zohar I 148a-148b,) which focuses on her evil and her murder of Eve's children after the break with Adam.

The Jewish folkloric myth of Lilith as the queen of the demons, wife of Satan (or of Samael, depending on the source) is almost identical to the Islamic Satan/Iblis myth. Lilith and the Islamic Satan/Iblis are both said to have defied God in exactly the same way – by refusing to bow down to Adam. The legend that is most popular today comes from the anonymous *Alphabet of Ben-Sira*, a Midrash-type commentary written in Aramaic and Hebrew sometime between the eighth and eleventh centuries. The section about Lilith describes her refusing to take the subservient role to Adam during sex: "She said, 'I will not lie below,' and he said, 'I will not lie beneath you, but only on top. For you are fit only to be in the bottom position, while I am to be the superior one.'" Lilith is then said to have uttered the ineffable name of God and flown away. The *Alphabet* is not regarded as seminal information in any other way – its portrayal of Joshua, who led the conquering Israelites into the Promised Land, describes him as a fat buffoon and King David is portrayed as a spiteful hypocrite – but when it comes to Lilith, it is the source of the theory that it all started in an argument about dominance in sex.

Both Lilith's anger and her punishment for leaving Adam are said to take many horrific forms. She is said to have married Satan/Samael, and to have sworn to destroy the children of her rival Eve. To this day, in orthodox Jewish homes, tokens of the angels Senoi, Sansenoi and Sannangelof are placed in the rooms of new-born children to protect them from Lilith's vengeance – and Lilith's own children are doomed to immediate destruction. Lilith is immortal, having never eaten from the Tree of Knowledge and putting on the "coat of skin" of the physical world as Adam and Eve did.

The legend is that the first woman refused to bow to the first man. This was a refusal to "prostrate" herself before him. Some say God commanded her to do so, others that Adam commanded her. Spanish Sephardi Jewish versions of the story say she wanted his power as well as her own. This refusal to bow and the wanting of Adam's power as well as her own are the aspects of women which are still feared in "powerful" women today. As might be expected, the idea that she refused to go below him during sex is the one which has taken precedence in modern interpretations and, frankly, there is a lot of feminist bunk written in defence of Lilith.

The fall

But the story is also open to a radical, new interpretation. Kabbalah teaches that when God created the Universe he did so through ten vessels known as *Sefirot* (Hebrew for circle or sapphire but generally translated as "vessel"). One of the vessels was filled with Divine light and when it was full, it overflowed to the next vessel. So, each vessel when completed, bowed in order to fill another.

In the Eastern countries of the world, it is the great masters who bow first to their students, and the host and hostess who bow to the guests coming into their homes. They are not bowing because they are inferior but because they are acknowledging the Divinity in the other person. If the Dalai Lama should bow to you, you would see it as a sign of his great stature, compassion and spiritual humility, not as a sign of weakness.

This interpretation changes the whole tenor of the story. Lilith was asked to bow to Adam. Had she understood the command, she would happily have bowed to Adam, passing on the light and power flowing in to her from God and knowing that it was not a command to be – or go – beneath him. Contemporary, psychological interpretation of this aspect of the legend implies that Lilith's behaviour stemmed directly from her own feelings of worthlessness. She believed that she *was* less than Adam. It was her lack of faith in her own beautiful feminine power and her own Divinity which made her see him as superior and to interpret the command to bow to him as proving her inferiority. Perhaps she did try to steal his power to fill the void she thought she had inside her. The great tragedy is that she never saw that doing so was quite unnecessary.

That was the fall. It had nothing to do with apples.

The legend of the temptation of Eve also bears a different interpretation from the more commonplace idea of the "fall from Grace". It has been used for centuries as a rod with which to beat women – even as far back as the beginning of the second century the Early Church Father, Tertullian, wrote to the female members of the Christian community in Carthage saying, "You are the devil's gateway…you are she who persuaded him whom the devil did not dare attack … Do you not know that you are each an Eve? The sentence of God on your sex lives on in this age; the guilt, necessarily, lives on too."

For many Catholics, the Virgin Mary represents the redemption of Eve (as in Kabbalistic teaching, Esther is the redemption of Lilith). St John Chrysostom, writing in the fourth century, went so far as to say that Eve's sin was such that woman was no longer formed in God's image and even Mary's excellence is not enough to overcome that. With respect to an ancient and revered saint, that is a supposition based on sheer ignorance of the Jewish tradition at the time that the Old Testament was written down.

Unfortunately, many people still hold such a view.

This book is not about reacting to misogyny, but it is important to point out yet again a key difficulty, as explained by the renowned Jewish Bible expert Claude Montefiore in *A Rabbinic Anthology* (Philadelphia, 1960):

"Rabbinic literature is written by men and for men... it is true the rabbis were almost always monogamists; it is true that they honored their mothers profoundly, and usually honored and cared for their wives. But that is only one side of the story.

'Women, children and slaves': that familiar and frequent collocation means and reveals a great deal. Women were, on the whole, regarded as inferior to men in mind, in function and status."

But this was only the view of religious men of the times. It is not the truth, the whole truth and nothing but the truth.

A threat

Humans usually only deride things that they see as a threat. Where the written tradition is generally male, an oral teaching, based on the wisdom of the Earth would be seen as feminine, uncontrollable and therefore threatening. As we have seen, the women carried secrets of healing and herbal medicine and life and death. This conferred mystery, power and inspiration that the men's pre-ordained, unchangeable services could not emulate. And, if the women, as well as having their own secrets, also wanted to have the men's ceremonies and initiatory rites (as Lilith wanted Adam's power as well as her own), who would blame the men for being angry or for feeling dispossessed? From such feelings of being under threat from something powerful, it would be easy to be goaded into a witch-hunt. And that is probably just what happened.

However, it is worth looking at the sayings of the Midrash to see what the rabbinic opinion was written down as being. The Midrash says, in its commentary on the story of Abraham and Sarah, that women have four main traits. They are greedy, eavesdroppers, slothful and envious. The rabbis then add three more traits – accusing women of being talkative, scratchers, prone to steal and with a tendency towards "gadding about". The complete and total evidence of these eight sins is as follows:

Eve was greedy: "She took of the fruit thereof and did eat." (Genesis 3:6).

Sarah was an eavesdropper: "and Sarah heard in the tent door." (Genesis 17:10)

And she was slothful – Abraham had to command her to "make ready quickly three measures of fine meal." (Genesis 18:6)

She was a scratcher "my scratch be upon thee." Note, this is a rabbinical misinterpretation of a Hebrew word *hamasi* – my wrong –being derived from *himmes*, to scratch. The correct Biblical translation is *my wrong be upon thee* (Gen 16:5)

Rachel was envious: "Rachel envied her sister." (Genesis 30:1)

And prone to steal "and Rachel stole the images." (Genesis 31:19)

Miriam was talkative: "and Miriam spoke against Moses." (Numbers 12:1)

Dinah, Leah's daughter, was a gadabout: "and Dinah went out." (Genesis 34:1)

The commentaries also make much of the virtues of the women, but because these are generally related to good wives or mothers, they are mostly discounted nowadays. In fact each of the women mentioned has a great character of her own and her weaknesses and faults are what make her interesting. The whole of the Old Testament is a document of the inward development of women, starting with the first mistake and ending with Esther, the humble Jewish girl who became a Queen and saved her people.

More sayings from the Midrash just prove how politically incorrect these rabbis were. But that was the way it was then. The interesting thing is that interpretations can be made in any age, according to that age, and it is, obviously, time for new interpretations on old but sound structures.

The Midrash asks: Why were so many of the Matriarchs barren? The answer is given as this:

"Because the Holy One, blessed be He, yearns for our prayers and supplications. So that they might lean on their husbands in spite of their beauty. So that they might pass the greater part of their life untrammelled. So that their husbands might derive pleasure from them for when a woman is with child she is disfigured and lacks grace. Thus the whole ninety years that Sarah did not bear, she was like a bride in her canopy."

Incidentally there was also a belief among the rabbis that a woman cannot conceive on having sex for the first time. In the cases where this actually happens in the Bible, they explain it as having resulted from a special act of will-power on the behalf of the woman – so imputing huge power of will onto the feminine.

It's all a bit self-centred and childish but you can bet that had women been writing down their views on men at the same time, they would not have been any more generous. You only have to listen to a group of women bemoaning their men to realise that this is not just a one-way street – and it never has been.

Choices and decisions

Eve is an easy scapegoat for everyone – her story comes right at the beginning of the Bible and she disobeys God. Rarely is she credited for being the first human being to make a free will decision which, for humanity's development, was itself profound. It was Eve who gave humanity the lesson of cause and effect. In doing so, she fell down. A human child today who tries to walk on its own and falls down, is not condemned but taught how to walk more safely. It is humanity which has condemned Eve, not her Father, no matter how it may look at first reading.

Adam and Eve may have understood the command not to eat of the Tree of Knowledge intellectually, but they had no knowledge of the idea of cause and effect or of wisdom. They were children living in a perfect world where everything else was permitted to them. Not one decision was necessary in order to live a happy life. To eat or not to eat from the Tree of Knowledge of Good and Evil was the first, possible choice and, like any child, Eve could not see why that choice should not be made. It didn't make sense.

Kabbalistic legend tells that the Garden of Eden was not a physical world but paradise as we would experience it before birth or after death – a place of the soul not the body. After Eve had taken and eaten of the fruit and Adam had eaten too, God told them that their disobedience meant that they had to leave the paradise of Eden and descend into the physical world (putting on "coats of skin" – Gen 3:21) and therefore live physical lives which automatically included pain and death. They could only live in that world by constantly making choices and the lesson was to teach them clearly of the importance of each and every choice they made. That is still the lesson for us today.

The Kabbalistic oral tradition teaches that God knew perfectly well what would happen and that the whole idea was a set-up. All good advice for parents teaches that if there is a particular toy that is dangerous to a young child, it must be placed out of reach. And any parent knows what would happen if a toddler were left alone in a room full of toys, having been told that they can play with every single toy except one particularly beautiful one. Humanity had to fall to learn about understanding and choice so we could kick-start the wheel of life. Understanding that what Eve did was not wrong or evil but a part of every human being's experience of childhood, is an important key to understanding the inner teachings of the Bible.

Knowledge

In the anonymous Holy Grail Writings which inspired Mallory's *Morte d'Arthur*, the writer says that Eve did, finally, understand what was happening as Adam and she left Eden. She had pulled a twig and a leaf from the Tree of Knowledge as she took the fatal fruit, and she planted it as soon as she set foot on Earth to remind her, and the rest of humanity, of the way back to the heavens. This young Tree of Knowledge was the sign outside Eden of how to find the way to the Tree of Life, the other tree that grew in the centre of Paradise. It grew and flourished and the fruit of its offspring was said to be the source of food for Noah, his family and the animals, after the great flood destroyed everything else.

From Eve's tree was cut a staff which was passed down through generations until it was given to Moses by his wife Zipporah, one of the spiritual lineage carriers of the female line and the daughter of his teacher in the desert, Jethro. It was called the staff of sapphires. Today, that staff of sapphires is reflected in a Christian Bishop's crook (and in the crook of the Good Shepherd) but it also refers to the vessels of the Tree of Life and turns up in all kinds of books and myths including the Book of Mormon. There is much confusion as to whether it comes from the Tree of Knowledge or the Tree of Life but, perhaps, after the fall the two are the same.

Whichever it is, the staff still calls us back to the parent tree in the same way that the famous wardrobe of C. S. Lewis' story *The Lion, the Witch and the Wardrobe* was the doorway into the mystical world of

Narnia. That wardrobe was made from wood from the Narnian Tree of Life – which was planted from an apple that was taken (with permission) by the hero, Digory, from a celestial Tree of Life in order to offer protection to the new land of Narnia. It needed protecting from the witch Jadis, a descendent of Lilith.

The Chronicles of Narnia also carry the ultimate redemption of humanity in that world through the willingness of the Christ-figure, Aslan, to be sacrificed for the sins of mankind. It is the Lilith figure who commits the murder in those books and the male lion who is resurrected. But, just as in the Bible there are women who are a vital part of the story all along the way and although the men are the ones who fight the battles, it is Lucy, later High Queen of all Narnia for all time, who is the one to be given the cordial of life for the healing of the sick and dying.

CHAPTER SEVEN

JESUS AND THE VIRGIN – GOD AND GODDESS

Although she did not find bearing children as easy as her mother, Tamar gave birth to a son the following year. They called him Yohan and, although his birth was difficult and Tamar slow to recover, she was almost immediately pregnant with their second child.

Sarah's birth, however, was hard; Judith thought she had lost her daughter twice during the labour and the baby was not strong. Tamar was only seventeen but Judith knew that it was time to start taking care of her daughter's life and ensure that she had as few further pregnancies as possible.

Yeshua was consulted – strictly speaking, this was woman's business, but Tamar knew that she could tell her husband that efforts were being made to ensure that she survived at the cost of further children.

"Whatever preserves my wife's life," he said, smiling at her. She was resting in Judith and Susannah's place in her old home, still in the post-birth separation time when husband and wife were not supposed to touch. Tamar began to cry; she was worried about Sarah and still in some pain from the birth. Yeshua hesitated and then came to a decision. He crossed the room and put his arms around his wife in front of the other women. "Lean on me," he said. "I am here."

Judith and Susannah were shocked but pleased and a little envious. It was a break with convention but it was good to see a man understanding how his wife felt. Neither of their own husbands would have been comfortable with the conversation or broken the taboo. People could easily hide behind the laws of segregation, and although giving partners space to breathe kept some marriages strong, it could also cause discomfort.

Yeshua and Tamar were discussing this with Judith one summer afternoon while Tamar was nursing Sarah in the warmth of the sun. Yeshua's work for that week was finished and he and Tamar were debating whether to go to Nazareth a day early. By now, Yeshua was one of the minyon at the synagogue; his knowledge of the faith was strong and sound and he was an able support to the ageing rabbi. He was known too for his exceptional ability to interpret the law and apply what he called "greater laws". He would explain these to anyone who wanted to know – that the law of preservation of life was paramount and over-ruled all other laws. And that life included spiritual, home and emotional life not just physical existence. For someone to live a life that was not worth living for the sake of a law was not the Lord's will, he would say.

However, he was not in favour of breaking the law for no reason other than wilfulness. "The law is there for a reason," he said. "We are ignorant and, if we do not think and apply proper judgement and kindness to our actions, then we need the law to protect us from ourselves."

"So we know which laws to break?" said Judith in amazement.

"In a way. Certainly to know when a law is inappropriate," he said.

Yeshua often told stories to try and make himself clear. This was the story he told on that occasion.

When the Lord God said to the angels, "Let us make humankind in our image," the Angel of loving-kindness agreed, saying, "Let Man be created, because he will do acts of loving-kindness." The Angel of Truth said, "Don't create humankind because they will tell falsehoods and live false lives." The Angel of Judgement said, "Let humankind be created because he will do acts of charity," and the angel of Peace said, "Don't create humankind because he is entirely quarrelsome."

After the Lord God had heard the claims of both sides, He agreed with the Angels of Loving-kindness and Judgement and cast Truth to the ground.' (Zohar vol. 1 Perush HaSulam)

"But truth is truth!" said Judith, shocked.

"But what is truth?" asked Yeshua. "The truth is the same as the law. It is what has been decided before this day. But this day may require a new decision. If that decision is taken with judgement and loving-kindness it cannot harm the truth. The Lord wants us to consider the justice and the kindness in a truth before we accept it without question.

But it must be a balance between the two. If a new truth is made with just judgement – or with just loving-kindness, then it is a false truth and it will end up hurting us."

"You're too clever for me," laughed Judith and Tamar knew she disagreed. Tamar herself didn't fully understand but she knew that Yeshua was passionate about his learning and teaching. Sometimes that passion frightened her and she knew that he felt restless at times and wanted to spend time in Jerusalem and other cities learning even more from the sages who knew and understood about judgement and loving-kindness.

As well as having work to do in Sepphoris, and wanting to be with each other, both Tamar's and Yeshua's families took a great deal of their time. Their home in Sepphoris was surrounded by family members and their children, and it was no different in Nazareth. Yeshua's four brothers – Yacob, Yoses, Simon and Yuda – all had families of their own as did his sisters, Mary and Salome. The town was filled with dozens of cousins, nieces, nephews as well as Miriam's own parents, cousins and more distant relations. Yeshua's father, Yosef, died just before Sarah was born – to the grief of all – but he too had brothers and cousins, all of whom had children. It seemed as if all of Nazareth was populated by Yeshua's family and Tamar never learnt the names of all of them.

She grew to love the visits to Nazareth after first resenting and then being too tired and sick to enjoy them. Firstly, this was because of Miriam who was always surrounded by children and women but who somehow always found a few precious moments to listen and understand the younger woman's problems. Like her first-born son, Miriam had some kind of special space within her; a space of peace and compassion. Not that she could not be fierce; once she found her grandson, Andrew, *tormenting a baby bird and he felt the full weight of a formidable anger. But there was a comforting space around Miriam where you could feel very safe.*

The second reason for loving Nazareth was the land itself. Unlike Sepphoris where every inch was filled with people and possessions, in Nazareth there was space to spread out. The family small-holding, just outside the town, was run by Yuda and his children but everyone helped out because it was the family's main source of prosperity and food. There was a chance to work with fruits and vegetables in the sunshine; a place where the children could run and shout without disturbing people and a place where the miracles of flowers, fruits and vegetables growing could be observed and harvested.

As well as the Nazareth connection, there was Yohan, son of Miriam's cousin Elisabeth and her husband Zechariah. They lived near Jerusalem in a village called Eim Karem but Yohan, now he was grown up, spent much of his time travelling in the Galilee region. Yohan was Yeshua's special friend but the other family members found him too strange for comfort. He was an ascetic, a Nazarite and fiercely religious – and he had never married. That was strange and confusing to most normal people. He was as stern as Yeshua was forgiving and most of the women and children were slightly afraid of him.

"I don't understand why you want to spend so much time with him," Tamar said pettishly when Yeshua excused himself from a family gathering to go walking with Yohan.

"Because we argue!" said Yeshua with a grin. "I can't argue with the rabbis in Sepphoris but I can argue all day with Yohan. And talk to Abba with him in a different way. It's hard to explain, I'm sorry... I wish I could."

But she did understand. Yohan and Yeshua were different from the others. They called the Lord Abba – "Daddy" – instead of "Father" and although Yohan's prayer was imperious and Yeshua's more like having a chat, they were equally different from everyone else. Yohan was unsettling; Yeshua was comforting and unsettling simultaneously and often Tamar found herself defending him against the less-religious-minded members of the family.

The family's choices of argument were the same as any other tight-knit group's – who should do what; how each should behave to the other and discussions of all kinds of social gossip from within the town and, sometimes, from Jerusalem. Herod was held in disdain by all and the Romans were cordially hated and despised especially for their pagan and heretical beliefs. Their gods and goddesses were thought pathetic and ineffectual and the clothing of their women disgraceful and immodest. The boys of the families, of course, enjoyed watching Roman women when they saw them, and an ankle, arm or bare-head caused giggles and cat-calls that were rewarded with a clip around the ear from their fathers, if they were caught in the act.

Although Tamar did not understand her husband's faith she knew that it was a vital part of him. One day Miriam acknowledged Tamar's support, in a way that made her daughter-in-law feel very special.

"I always knew that you were the one he needed as a wife," she said. "You are the only one who could love him and understand him. You do love him, don't you?"

"Yes," said Tamar, shyly. Love was not expected or talked of much in marriage, only in regard to feelings for children.

"He knows that; he knows that he is free to be himself with you," said Miriam. "See the difference between him and Yacob?" Yacob was Yeshua's nearest brother in age. He was married to Rachel and had six children.

"But Yacob isn't interested in study like Yeshua is," said Tamar. "He's always with the family."

"Yes, he is interested," said Miriam. "But Rachel isn't; she thinks it's a waste of time and he does not over-rule her."

"Well they have more responsibilities than we do," said Tamar, uncomfortably aware of her very small family.

"It is all meant," said Miriam, taking her hand. "But even if you had six children, you would still be Tamar and you would still see that Yeshua is the better father and husband for being able to study and follow his heart. I am so grateful to you, Tamar. Thank you very much."

After this, Tamar watched Yacob and Rachel carefully. She saw the discord between them and how Rachel fought every movement Yacob would make to be with his brother. She was jealous! It was understandable, but with the wisdom she had learnt over the years, Tamar could begin to see that Rachel's control only harmed her marriage; the time that Yacob spent with her when he would rather have been with Yeshua and Yohan was not good time. Yes, Tamar had less time with her husband but when he was there, his entire attention was with her, their Yohan and Sarah.

Both families had quite enough in resources and talents to live comfortably but not enough to live a life of luxury. Yeshua and Tamar did not have the extra money that would have been needed for Yeshua to travel to Jerusalem to continue his studies. He had out-grown all his teachers in Sepphoris and Tamar knew he had itchy feet. But there seemed to be nothing that could be done.

But one day, when Yohan was having a rough-and-tumble in the olive groves outside Nazareth with his cousins Levi and David, Tamar looked at the discontented face of Rachel as she came to fetch her children and had a sudden realisation of how very blessed she was in her life, her children and her husband.

"I wish I could help him," she thought. "I would willingly let him go to Jerusalem if I could raise the money. But I have no means to help him."

The old story of judgement and loving-kindness came back to her then and she sat back on her heels. It was true that she could not help – but maybe there was a different truth as well. This thought was strange and unsettling and she felt uncomfortable. But it would not go away.

"Then how?" she asked, in a silent prayer to a God she never really bothered with much. She relied on Yeshua to pray for her. Yes, she had her

images hidden in their little home, she went to synagogue and she kept the laws, but unless she were in pain or fear, she did not speak to the Lord on her own.

Yohan jumped on her, knocking back her veil. With a crow of delight he seized one of her long, black plaits and pulled it really hard. Tamar had an idea...

Three nights later, back in Sepphoris, when the children were asleep and she and Yeshua were about to go to bed themselves, Tamar nervously handed her husband a pouch containing money.

"To go to Jerusalem to study – when you are able," she said.

Yeshua looked at her in astonishment. Then he took the pouch and looked inside.

"What have you done?" he asked. "How did you get this?"

In answer, Tamar pushed back her veil showing a tousled head of short, curly hair. She had had the long plaits cut off and sold them.

"Your beautiful hair!" said Yeshua. "Tamar, your beautiful hair!"

"A woman should only show her hair to her husband," said Tamar. "It is the law. So I wanted to show you how much I love you by having it cut so you can go and study as you truly want to. I think that's right," she added a little nervously. "No one will know but you and me. It was judgement and loving-kindness – I think – rather than just truth."

"Oh you best of wives," said Yeshua. "Oh most blessed of women. Thank you so very, very much."

Peter

When the focus of the Christian faith moved to Rome along with the apostles Peter and Paul, Roman beliefs and ethics overcame the basic Jewish tenets with which Christianity had begun. Even more, the great goddess cults, particularly that of Vesta, who equates with the Jewish Shekhinah, began to influence Christianity. Nowadays, it is complete Catholic dogma that Jesus had no blood-brothers or sisters and that his mother, Mary, was a virgin from birth to death. This belief would have been impossible in Jewish Christianity; it was contrary to the teachings of the Torah.

Christianity, like history, is taught by the winners. The winners were the Romans, particularly under the third century Constantine.

Although the Acts of the Apostles makes it clear that it was Jesus' brother Yacob (called James in the New Testament) who became the leader of the apostles after the resurrection, there is no image of James in the images of church leaders in the Church of St Paul, built on Paul's alleged tomb, just outside of Rome. He is not acknowledged as the first Pope – Peter has that title.

The Biblical reason for this are Jesus' words to Peter "Thou art Peter, and upon this rock I will build my church." (Matthew 16:18). And yet, just five verses later, comes this: "He turned, and said unto Peter, Get thee behind me, Satan; thou art an offence unto me; for thou savourest not the things that be of God, but those that be of men." For the Greek scholar, in particular, it is painfully clear that Peter just didn't get it. He had no comprehension of Jesus' actual teaching, even if he did recognise him as the Anointed One.

This failing is clearly seen in the passage in John 21:15 where the resurrected Jesus asks Peter three times if he loves him. Three times, Peter answers yes, becoming more and more aggrieved that Jesus would ask him the same question more than once. But for most of this discussion, Jesus and Peter are using entirely different words for love and Peter is completely unable to distinguish between the two. Jesus speaks of *agapeo* or spiritual love and Peter answers with *phileo*, family love. So the conversation goes: "Peter do you love me spiritually (i.e. beyond the personal)?" and the answer is "Yes, Lord, I love you personally." The third time of asking, Jesus also uses the word *phileo* because he realizes that Peter cannot understand what he is trying to say.

Mary

Even if the Christian church had been founded entirely on Peter's belief, it is unlikely that it would have become a place of the veneration of virginity. Peter had a wife – as mentioned previously. St Paul won the first battle as to how Christianity would be shaped. Even though he never met Jesus and all his inspiration came from personal revelation, he was clear that it was better to remain unmarried if you could. He did write the earliest texts known but, interestingly, he mentions nothing about Mary's virginity; in Galatians he describes Jesus as born of a woman not a virgin. He makes no mention of Judas' betrayal either. The gospels of Mark (the first written) and John do not talk about Mary's virginity either. However, as the development of Christianity expanded, the concept of Jesus' divinity became more and more important and the best way to show Jesus as son of God was to promote Mary's virginity.

St Jerome even claimed that Joseph had a brother whose wife was also called Mary and that *their* children were the ones who were referred to as the brothers and sisters of Christ. This ignores the evidence that the Greek words used for Jesus' brothers and sisters is *adelphos* which, although it can have a wider meaning, is more likely to mean child of the same parents rather than *sugenos*, which means wider kin and is used for Mary's cousin Elisabeth.

It is fascinating to watch the editing out of Jesus' family as Christianity grew. James the Just, who is clearly outlined as Jesus' brother (Galatians 1:90), became Jesus' successor and formulated the faith's structure for the next 30 years. However, James was Jewish and the Christian drive in Rome was primarily Gentile. James ruled that Gentiles should be allowed to be a part of the faith without having to convert. It is very clear in the Acts of the Apostles that he, and the other original disciples, were most uncomfortable with Paul's version of Christianity.

Ironically, it is a gospel attributed to this very James which provided the ground-bed for the theory that Mary was a perpetual virgin. The Gospel of James, written around 150 CE portrays Jesus' earthly father Joseph as an ageing widower with existing children who was chosen as the husband for Mary, a divine child who was raised in the Temple but who had to leave that holy space once menstruation made her impure.

This Gospel of James even gets a woman called Salome to check Mary's vagina for virginity after the birth of Jesus. This would mean that she had given birth to a child without breaking her hymen (a caesarean birth would have been somewhat unlikely at that time).

It's important to say here that Kabbalah teaches that Divine power and authority would be perfectly capable of enabling a virgin to conceive. It is also very true that the Gospels refer to Christ as the "only begotten" of God. But they also make it clear that Jesus was Mary's first-born, the word used in Luke 2:7 is just that: *prototokos*. However, as the concept of Jesus Christ became more divine, so did his mother Mary and it became heretical to believe that she could ever have had sex.

Ironically, the Catholic Church in Spain and southern Europe unwittingly depicts Jesus and the Virgin Mary as husband and wife. Apart from the occasional statue of Mary at the foot of the cross, all her images in churches show a young woman with or without her baby – matched with an image of Jesus as a young man. Jesus is the husband and Mary the bride. Together, they are the Masculine Creative impulse and the Earth Goddess who bring life to the world.

It is the same in Christian art throughout the ages. An ancient and powerful truth translated through pagan lore has seeped into Christianity to make it a nature religion of re-creative life. The male and the female are united in Spring in order to give birth to the new year at the Winter Solstice – the Christian festival of Christmas. There is nothing wrong with this; it does not detract from the Christian story, rather it shows that it follows the great sacred path of life. All the great myths and truths of the world are basically the same story.

Until the Protestant reformation all of Christianity had a feminine aspect of God – Mary the Virgin – providing a vital balance to its masculinity. It is sometimes hard to remember that monotheism only spread throughout the world with the advent of Christianity. Before then, Judaism was not widely known outside the Holy Land and Islam had not yet been revealed.

In the ancient religions there were many goddesses and most polytheistic systems had a King and Queen of the Gods such as Jupiter and Juno; Zeus and Hera. Even Judaism placed – and still places – great emphasis on Shekhinah, the Presence of God, seen as the feminine aspect which gives birth to souls and receives them back after death. However, with the rise of Christianity and papal power, the pagan gods and goddesses slowly disappeared from Western culture. For the male gods it was not such a problem – many images of Jesus look very similar to Helios, the Greek god of the sun – and his powers are said to equal any of the other gods'. So great was devotion to the Goddess that She was resurrected in the hearts of the people by a new Goddess, Mary, Mother of Jesus, himself the Christian version of the Green Man.

Catholics emphasise that the Virgin Mary is the first of the saints but, as she was human, she is not worshipped. However, the adoration of the Virgin is a profound part of Catholic theology and the distinction is often hard for non-Catholics to understand. Mary is constantly asked to intercede for people in their prayers – as though she can and will persuade an unwilling son to soften his heart to our needs. That Mary was born and died a virgin is accepted as absolute truth throughout the Catholic Church. Catholics also believe that Mary was bodily assumed into heaven rather than suffering a physical death, and that she is honored as Queen there. The *Regina Coeli* (Queen of Heaven) is an anthem used in Catholic churches at Eastertime and, of course, she has her own prayer, the *Ave Maria* (Hail Mary) which is an important part of daily Catholic ritual. Mary was declared to be the "Mother of God" by the Christian church in the fifth century at Ephesus, Turkey, a place previously devoted to the worship of another great goddess, Artemis, who was also known as the Queen of Heaven.

Over the centuries, visions of the Virgin Mary have appeared to thousands of people – especially to children – around the world. Her best-known sacred shrines are at Lourdes in France, Fatima in Portugal and

Guadalupe in Mexico. Even now, the Internet carries stories of her image appearing in places that range from the sublime to the ridiculous. In November 2004 a toasted cheese sandwich said to bear an image of the Virgin Mary sold on the eBay auction website for $28,000. An internet casino purchased the sandwich from its physical maker, Diane Duyser from Florida, USA, saying it had become a part of pop culture.

Since 1894, Catholic dogma has asserted that the soul of the Virgin Mary was conceived without the stigma of original sin and that she lived an Earthly life completely free from sin. This idea of Immaculate Conception is freqently confused with the idea of virgin birth, but it actually refers to the state of Mary's soul; her conception and birth were biologically normal. The Feast of the Immaculate Conception was originally an Eastern Catholic festival, first celebrated in the West in the eighth century and established as fact by Pope Sixtus IV in 1476. However, it was not asserted as dogma – i.e. it *must* be believed – until defined by Pope Pius IX in 1854. As late as 1950 the Roman Catholic Church issued the dogma that Mary's body was assumed into heaven at her death. This was based on a fifth century text known as the Transitus Mariae which was originally ruled to be a heresy.

The Madonna and child image also pre-dates Christianity. In many European countries, the melding of the ancient Earth Goddess with the Virgin Mary has been unofficially acknowledged for centuries. The Madonna, whether she is known as Isis cradling Horus, or Mary cradling Jesus, or Demeter cradling Persephone/Kore or Cybele cradling Attis embodies Female Divinity for many millions of people. The list of mother-goddesses is virtually endless and they all appear to merge: Ninlil, wife of Enlil in ancient Sumer, evolved into Ishtar of Babylon, Dushara of Phoenicia, and Allat and Lato of Greece and Rome. Even the shrines are in the same places; people visit Ephesus to visit the house of the Virgin Mary just as they once visited the nearby, now-destroyed temple of Artemis.

Artemis herself, like many of the ancient goddesses, is an enigma; in some places she was a multi-breasted mother goddess and in others, a virgin huntress. In Scythia (now Kazakhstan, southern Russia and eastern Ukraine) there were warrior-women who may have been the basis for the myth of Amazons. They worshipped the huntress Artemis, who was the goddess usually associated with the Amazons, and early forms of her worship involved both animal and human sacrifice. Artemis Tauropolis (also known as Taurica Dea on the island of Tauris in the Black Sea) demanded the sacrifice of male prisoners who had been shipwrecked. Their throats were cut; they were then decapitated and dropped over a cliff. In another sacrificial rite, various animals were burned alive. In other places, like Aricia in Italy, Artemis/Diana had a grove which was a sanctuary of peace where women came to pray for easy childbirth.

Diana had another grove at Tibur (now Tivoli) where she was called Opifera, meaning "bringer of help" – and Opifera was also one of the names of Bona Dea, the "good goddess", who, together with Diana and Demeter/Ceres was a protector of the oppressed classes, especially the enslaved.

The goddess Vesta, however, is different. She was a virgin goddess of the hearth, home and family and is the goddess closest in comparison to Mary – both virgin and in charge of the home. Her equivalent in Greek mythology was Hestia. To the Romans, the Vestal Virgins represented guardians both of their purity and their family life. Their celibacy was the sacrifice offered to Vesta for the health and fertility of Rome's citizens. As goddess of the Hearth, Vesta was represented in every home by the wife (her husband represented Janus, god of the doorway). She was the symbol of the home, around which a newborn child must be carried before it could be received into the family. Vesta was particularly important to women as the hearth was the place where food was prepared and next to it the meal was eaten with offerings being thrown into the fire to seek omens from how they burned. In a religiously-minded household, every meal began and ended with an offering to Vesta and this prayer:

Vesta, in all dwellings of men and immortals
Yours is the highest honor, the sweet wine offered
First and last at the feast, poured out to you duly
Never without you can gods or mortals hold banquet.

Vesta has no distinct personality, plays no part in the myths and is never depicted in an image or a statue; the sacred flame was her symbol just as the lighting of the candles in a Jewish household on the Sabbath Eve is the presence of Shekhinah.

There is one thing that differentiates Mary from all these goddesses; the way in which she is worshipped. She is only meant to be revered: no sacrifices are made in her name and no sexual festivals are held in her honor. However, like Cybele, her priests are voluntarily self-castrated (although not physically); like Diana, she is the source of prayer for women wanting children or safe childbirth; and like Demeter, Isis and Cybele she is the mother of the Divine Child. As with the other mother-goddesses, it is to Mary that many Catholics turn in order to beg her to intercede for them.

Judaism regards Christianity as a pagan religion because of its representation of Jesus as God and the reverence of the Virgin. To Jews, the images in Catholic churches or on the roof of the Sistine Chapel are a violation of the second commandment "no graven image" and, when you think of the countless people who truly believe that God is an old man in the sky looking down on us in judgement you can can see, perhaps, why the commandment was given. Once we have a "graven image" – that is to say an acknowledged "this is how it is" image – then it is almost impossible for us to comprehend God as a direct force in our lives, a spiritual essence or an impartial source of good.

Pope John Paul II was devoted to the Virgin Mary: his motto, *Totus Tuus* (totally yours), was dedicated to her and his personal coat of Arms contained the letter "M", representing Mary at the foot of the Cross.

We need the Goddess to match with the God. As stated already, ancient Jewish tradition teaches that Shekhinah is the feminine aspect balancing the masculine aspect of Adonai (the Lord). The other aspects of God have no sex at all and, if Jesus were not presented as Adonai we would be more comfortable with the idea of a sexless God. As it is, Shekhinah in the form of the Virgin Mary, is needed to create an essential balance.

If she is not there, we must look elsewhere. To Mary Magdalene.

CHAPTER EIGHT

JESUS' TEACHINGS ON MARRIAGE

Yohan grew steadily and Sarah survived all the illnesses of childhood, a little weak and frail and prone to coughs and colds, but her father's darling. Tamar remained strong without the pressures of childbirth and the little family was a happy one, weathering the storms and silences, joys and tragedies of their kin and the society around them.

Yeshua spent six months in Jerusalem and came home thinner but very happy. He was subtly changed; a holy man indeed and one who spoke less but more to the point. It took a little time for both of them to re-adjust to married life and they had to face much jibing about Yeshua's so-called religious fervour and his refusal to come home to his wife each Sabbath Eve.

"The spirit of the law, not the letter of the law," they would say to each other under their breaths, with a kiss, every time the outer world tried to make them feel wrong.

Yeshua and Tamar were a good team, understanding each other and growing in love with each year that passed. They had their ups and downs; their little issues and their simmering quarrels, but at the root of it all was, always, the teaching of discernment and loving-kindness.

Tamar grew wise and respected in the community; she helped other women through the trials of learning how to be a wife and a mother. Many were the women who thanked her for calling them to task to find the origin of a quarrel between them and their husbands – so that it could be healed at the source. She never berated her sisters but she taught them how to learn from the story of Eve to make themselves stronger.

Yeshua and Tamar had sixteen years together – a good life. Tamar did conceive again three times – and miscarried (with help from the local herbalists). She lived just long enough to see her son, Yohan, married to a fine, good-hearted girl. He grew to be an upright strong young man – a glassmaker like his grandfather. Sarah too was betrothed to an older man whose wife had died and who already had children. Tamar worried for her but the girl was sensible for all her fragility and she knew how to take care of her body.

It was at Yohan's wedding that Tamar realised she was pregnant again. She sought advice as before but this time the herbs did not work. Judith, still strong and active, nursed her daughter lovingly and tried to hide her concern. But even Yeshua's prayers and the warm healing effect of his hands on her abdomen at night could not help her this last time. Tamar began to haemorrhage in her fifth month and the bleeding would not stop.

In the very last hour, with her mother's poppy syrup dissolving the pain, she lay weak but sleepily conscious on the bed. Yeshua sat with her, his always spare body yet thinner from lack of food. He could not stomach anything while she was suffering.

There was no thought now about the impurity in touching a woman who bled. For a moment she remembered back to the very beginning of their marriage and smiled.

"We have done well," she said. "We have been happy."

"Yes," he said, quietly. "Very happy."

They were silent again, both accepting the situation; there was nothing that could be done and it was the way of life. Again she found herself amused. He had no doubts that she would continue to exist in some fashion after her physical life was over; that God and his angels would come to fetch her. That would be nice, she thought. But if not, then sleep will also be good...

"You should take better care of yourself," she said suddenly, rousing herself. "I can't leave you to starve in a world of plenty, where sisters, daughters and mothers are fighting over who should feed you."

He smiled back but said nothing.

"Wait until Sarah is safely married," she said, tightening her grasp on

his hand. *"Before you go."*

"Go?"

"Yes, you know you have a destiny; even if it wasn't there in your eyes, even if you didn't hanker after cousin Yohan's life of teaching, your mother told me."

"Ah," he stroked the back of the work-roughened but now translucent hand holding tightly onto his. *"I would rather it was not like this."*

"Better this way," she said. *"I have been so happy, but there is work for you to do and I would be in the way."*

"Never," he said, raising the hand and kissing it. *"Best of wives; best of mothers; best of friends."*

She slipped into unconsciousness; a great feeling of peace overwhelming her. The last recognisable image was a dappling of light in her eyes as if the wing of some great bird had crossed the sun above her. All care dissolved. Had she been able to catch her thoughts she might have thought she heard the words *"Well done, thou good and faithful servant,"* but she would not have known who spoke them. Tamar died in her husband's arms – he would not leave her although the women begged him to go out of the room as was customary. At the moment that she died, he bent his head over her body and wept.

They buried her at sunset that day; wrapped in a linen shroud and watered with the tears of many who loved her. For weeks, Yeshua went to her grave every day and left a stone. He never ceased to pray.

The death of Sarah, their pale, beautiful and gentle daughter, from a fever three months later struck another terrible blow. He had carried her on his shoulders until her thirteenth year for she was always a tiny little thing. Tamar's death broke something in Sarah and she was not strong enough to beat another illness. This kind, God-fearing, God-loving man bent but did not break under the grief. He knew that life as he had known it was over and it was time to make another beginning.

Once he had carried his beloved child's body to the grave she would share with her mother, he handed his business into the care of his family, *cut his hair and took the Nazarite vow for three months. Sometimes the family were almost afraid of him as he would sit for hours on end either in the synagogue or by the side of the road. When he wasn't praying, he appeared to be listening.*

The vow completed, he walked to Nazareth to take leave of his mother, Miriam, who saw at once that his calling had come. Immune to the pleas of his brothers, sisters, cousins and friends, the man who would become known as Jesus of Nazareth stood, tall and strong and accepting of his mission from the Divine. Then, he walked to the river Jordan to find his cousin, John the Baptist.

Gospel evidence

The story of Jesus' life from the age of about 34 onwards is, traditionally, told in four Gospels – Matthew, Mark, Luke and John. As mentioned, although his birth date is usually thought to be the year zero, CE it is far more likely to have been about 5-6 BCE if the political facts given in the Gospel of Luke are true. This would mean that he had plenty of time to marry and raise a family before beginning his ministry.

There are many other Gospels besides the four best-known Biblical ones, but these have formed what is known as the Canon of the Church for more than 700 years. The Gnostic gospels, which were discovered in Nag Hammadi, Upper Egypt, in 1945 and other testaments discovered over the years add to the stories and put many different slants on them, but none contain such clear and compelling narratives of dates, places and times over three years of what, at first, appears to be a contradictory ministry.

Many of the of the Nag Hammadi scrolls were burnt just after their discovery because no one thought that they were valuable. Despite this, at least 50 alternative texts survive. Absolutely nothing that remains to us was written while Jesus was alive. Most of the work was written at least 100 years after his death and by people who had heard stories and had direct inspiration from above. The earliest possible dating for the first written Gospel, Mark, is 60 CE, a time when there might have been some eye-witnesses still living.

The Nag Hammadi scrolls were finally translated into modern language in the 1970s and they burst like wildfire into a secular world which was already questioning conventional Christianity and religion. The Dead Sea Scrolls, which were discovered in 1947 near Qumran in Israel, are equally controversial but they are not directly concerned with Jesus of Nazareth – they are believed to pre-date him – and in content they are less personal than the Gnostic Gospels. The Dead Sea Scrolls are still immensely valuable to scholars as they contain early copies of Biblical books in Hebrew and Aramaic, and writings attributed to ancient biblical characters such as Enoch or Abraham. Many of the texts are believed to be Essene, or similar in origin, but they do include similarities with teachings by other Jewish groups: the Sadducees, Pharisees and Zealots. Conspiracy theories say that some unpublished copies of the Scrolls reveal that the teachings of Jesus were around before he was born, therefore negating Jesus' position as the Messiah proclaiming a "new" truth. In fact, careful study of the Bible reveals that most of Jesus' teaching is based on Jewish belief. Where this is not obvious in the accepted Bible text, it is apparent through examination of what is known of the oral tradition of the ancient days – and in texts such as Nag Hammadi.

What people of faith often miss is that there is *always* an oral tradition that follows some great revelation or discovery. An "official" version is written down, but those who have ears to hear will know that it may be the truth and nothing but the truth, but it is not the *whole* of the truth. This must be discovered by the seeker. As Jesus himself says "do not cast pearls before swine" (Matt 7:6). If all the sacred knowledge of the world were written down for all to read, it would be misunderstood, misused and reviled. It certainly would not be valued if it were too easy to access. The spiritual seeker is like a child wanting to explore everything without realising that all actions have consequences. The original story of Adam and Eve is intended to let us know that all actions have consequences and if we break universal law, then it will rebound on us.

The Nag Hammadi scrolls are important in examining the relationship between Jesus and the feminine but not in examining marriage. Their attitude towards physical marriage varies. Some are as avid as the Catholic Church that celibacy and/or asceticism is to be preferred, but others extol the mysteries of marriage.

The Gospel of Philip and the Gospel of Mary are the primary sources of the theory that Jesus and Mary Magdalene were married. In the Gospel of Philip, Jesus is quoted as saying, "Great is the mystery of marriage! For without it the world would not have existed. Now the existence of the world depends on man, and the existence of man on marriage. Think of the undefiled relationship, for it possesses a great power. Its image consists of a defilement of the form."

The Gospel of Philip is believed to date back to the second half of the third century CE so it may have been written more than 200 years after Jesus lived. It's mostly a collection of sayings without a narrative and although most Gnostic writers think it of significant importance, other scholars disagree. Ian Wilson (*Jesus: The Evidence*, Harper SanFrancisco) goes so far as to say that it "seems to be merely a Mills and Boone-style fantasy of a type not uncommon among Christian apocryphal literature". It is the last sentence in the above excerpt from the Gospel of Philip that I find to be the most interesting. The "image" of marriage consists of a defilement of its "form." Here, Jesus appears to be saying that marriage is much misinterpreted and misunderstood and is meant to be undertaken with a higher purpose, and maybe reverence, than it is. That would certainly fit with the marriage mores of the time where the majority of relationships were forged for social, financial and tribal reasons rather than to ensure a partnership working in harmony for good. Romantic love, as expected in marriage today, would also have been regarded as an unsound reason for marriage. So it may be that Jesus is referring to the idea of Sacred Marriage – the union of humanity with God.

The four Gospels: different interpretations

The conventional Gospels are much clearer about Jesus' teachings on marriage in the physical world – and on the dissolution of marriage. These are not, as is often thought, simple denouncements of divorce. Rather, they show a very profound understanding of the psychological and emotional toll of divorce. First, though, we need to examine how the four Gospels can be interpreted mystically. Ancient Kabbalistic teachings explain that we humans exists at four levels – physical, psychological (or soul), spiritual and Divine. Each of those levels is represented by an element – Earth, Water, Air and Fire – and we draw on all of them at different times according to how we are feeling.

If the Gospel writers knew of the Kabbalistic tradition (research demonstrates this would appear to be so), then choosing four specific Gospels to form the essence of the New Testament could be a way in which Jesus' story could be told at these four different levels – literally, allegorically, spiritually and mystically.

For those who were happy with the overview of the story, then all the Gospels could be woven together in one narrative – as in a Nativity play with both the shepherds and the Magi appearing in the same story, or in a Passion Play with Jesus saying "My God, why has Thou forsaken me?" (Matthew 27:46) and "Father forgive them, they know not what they do," (Luke 23:32) in the same scene. But for those who were looking for a deeper significance, or who were familiar with the esoteric tradition of the time, the four Gospels would provide a feast of different interpretations – and a much deeper knowledge of our own selves at the same time.

As metaphors for human development, Matthew demonstrates the physical Jesus, Mark the psychological (soul) Jesus, Luke the spiritual Jesus and John the Divine Jesus – the Christ within all of us.

Matthew represents the Earthly world of reality. Matthew writes of earthly power, tribe and leadership, including the importance of the right bloodline in the family. He also highlights the physical concerns and challenges of everyday life on earth and refers to Jesus' physical kingship as Messiah. It is a very masculine account; Jesus' birth is told with the emphasis on Joseph's genealogy and Joseph's views, on the visit of the wise men with their physical gifts and on King Herod's fears over the birth of a physical King of the Jews and the consequent slaughter. Here, the temptations before Jesus in the desert are all physical: turn stones into food; put his life in danger to prove that God would save him; and the offer of the kingship of the world.

Mark represents the psychological world – the soul's world. This element of water demonstrates how fluid our thoughts and feelings are. It is at this soul level that we can choose whether or not to be separate from animals (the "wild beasts" in Mark's Temptation story) in that we can become aware of free will. It is through the soul that we decide to act for good or for evil. Jesus' temptation in Mark is a choice between his baser self and a higher level of consciousness where he may be in touch with angels. Interestingly, throughout Mark Jesus has to battle with his own emotions and, in some of the oldest Latin texts of Mark and also in the respected fifth century Greek Codex Bezae, he is said to become angry at times when his power or his willingness to heal are challenged. Mark's gospel is unique in this respect and clearly shows the development of Jesus himself through the human emotions.

Luke writes of the Spiritual world represented by the element of air. Luke's Gospel is a very balanced account of Jesus' life when it comes to masculine and feminine. It features many couples – or at least male and female working together – such as Joseph and Mary, Zechariah and Elisabeth, Simeon and Anna. It strongly features Jesus' mother and his female friends, and it contains 19 stories about women as compared to four or five in all the other Gospels. Doing so emphasises that this is the Spiritual perception of life – that the feminine is equal to the masculine. Woman's place in the physical and tribal worlds was deemed unimportant in the Jewish, Roman and Greek worlds of Jesus' time, but at the spiritual level, the feminine in Judaism was deeply respected. Luke's Gospel is the one that focuses on the Archangel Gabriel's visit to Mary; Mary's visit to

Elizabeth; on how Mary feels; how Mary wraps her baby in swaddling clothes and lays him in a manger. The emphasis is on family, marriage and communication, which works in tandem with Matthew's tribal aspects, showing a different perspective through the balancing of masculine with feminine.

For Jesus' temptation in the desert, Luke offers the same challenges as in Matthew, but in a different order. In Luke, Jesus is told first to command stone to be turned into bread, then given the opportunity to rule the world and, finally, ordered to challenge God to save him by throwing himself off the Temple in Jerusalem. In Matthew, he replies with answers from the written (physical) law and in Luke he takes a different stance, replying with God's own authority at the Spiritual level.

John's Gospel does not tell of any temptation; at the level of development he is writing about, humanity would have transcended worldly needs. This Gospel is of the Divine World represented by the element of fire. It tells of direct experience of God. There are no parables, similes or allegories; it is Jesus telling us straight, and many mystics believe it better read from the viewpoint of the Christ consciousness within one's self rather than as a story of an external being.

The Gospels' differences can be seen very clearly in the four accounts of the Passion:

> For Matthew and Mark, physical and emotional, the crucifixion is full of pain and anguish, but Luke and John are focused on the mystery and the clarity of a Divinely inspired right of passage.

Matthew, Mark and Luke, the Synoptic Gospels, write that the "veil of the Temple was rent" (Matthew 27:51, Mark 15:38, Luke 23:45) when Jesus died. In an ordinary death, Jewish mystics taught that the veils of the two lower worlds (Matthew and Mark) are opened to let the soul though to the spiritual world. In the case of a Messiah, *all three* lower veils (Matthew, Mark and Luke) are opened to give direct access to the Divine.

In Matthew the earth quakes, the rocks are rent and bodies rise from the graves; in Mark, darkness comes down during the crucifixion and in Luke the Sun is darkened.

In John there is no earthly reaction to Christ's death but there is immediate emphasis that the next day is the Sabbath – the holy day of the Jews – and that Jesus' body must be taken down because that is a day of Divine contemplation and sacred rest.

In the lower worlds of Jesus' body and psyche, as represented in Matthew and Mark, Jesus is depicted as crying out at his betrayal – his physical and psychological bodies reacting as any ordinary man would. "My God, my God, why hast thou forsaken me?"

In Luke, Jesus is able to see his crucifixion as impersonal. There is no judgement of it or other people's behaviour. "Father, forgive them; for they know not what they do …, into thy hands I commend my spirit."

In John, the crucifixion is represented simply as a necessary evil on the way to new life. Without Jesus' acceptance and acknowledgement of death, resurrection cannot occur. Jesus gives completion to his mother by giving her into John's care and gives himself willingly to death, purely as the next stage of his development as a Divine being. "It is finished."

Although the four worlds differ from each other, they also have links flowing through them. The physical Matthew also embraces the lower part of the psychological Mark. Mark in turn embraces the lower part of spiritual Luke (the human soul is said to be the place where the three lower worlds meet) and the higher part of Luke links into the Divine John. So each world can "talk" to the others and make connections.

Another way of understanding the Gospels in this way is to see them as examples of our own development in life, from the rules and regulations of childhood that keep us safe (Matthew) through our teenage years of finding ourselves (Mark) to the development of a wider understanding of how humanity works (Luke) and an understanding of our relationship with God, humanity and the Universe (John). Humans operate from all these levels and all are essential to our survival as a race but we react differently from each one.

Marriage and divorce in the Gospels

It is the same in the Gospels' teaching on marriage. At first sight they are dogmatic and, for centuries, the sayings have been treated as law. If Jesus never married then his words on marriage are either Divinely inspired – or the words of yet another unmarried marriage guidance counsellor. But if, as I believe, he was working from inspiration *and* from direct experience and observation, then the Gospels' teaching on marriage is directly related to our four different levels of existence. Viewed this way, his teachings can be demonstrated to offer very valid and thought-provoking judgements.

In New Testament Greek the word marriage means either to be given or be taken in marriage; there is no word to imply a joint agreement between equals. In Hebrew there are more than five different words used for a committed relationship between men and women ranging from *ba'al* (to rule over or possess), through *ownah* (conjugal rights) to *halal* (to shine, praise or be worthy – psalm 78) and *nasa* (to lift up – or to endure!). Mostly the couples are just referred to as dwelling together or being the male or female counterpart of the other. Interestingly, most marriages in Biblical days were secular, as they are today. Only the very religious asked for a rabbi's blessing on the ceremony, which, as we have seen, was more of a contract between families than an emotional agreement.

If a marriage is sanctified to God, it is then lifted to the spiritual world so that it can work at a level beyond family ties. The book of Genesis is clear that humans must leave their parents and "cleave" unto their spouse. However, just getting married in a church or synagogue does not mean that the couple has consciously sanctified the relationship in this way. Jesus only speaks of divorce in Matthew, Mark and Luke, the Synoptic Gospels, which are all believed to have been drawn from the same source. The source is either a vanished original manuscript, known to scholars as

"Q" or the oral tradition.

This is what Jesus says about marriage in the Gospel of Matthew:

> "It hath been said, 'Whosoever shall put away his wife, let him give her a writing of divorcement.' But I say unto you, 'That whosoever shall put away his wife, saving for the cause of fornication, causeth her to commit adultery; and whosoever shall marry her that is divorced committeth adultery.'
>
> His disciples say unto him, 'If the case of the man be so with a wife, it is not good to marry.' But he said unto them, 'All cannot receive this saying, save to whom it is given.'" (Matthew 5: 31)

When a couple breaks up there is an emotional fall-out as well as the physical dividing-up of belongings and the physical loss of bodily contact and connection. Here, Jesus is pointing out the difference between the physical adultery of sleeping with another person and the psychological break-up of a relationship for other reasons. Kabbalists and scientists view the meaning of the word "adultery" as "to mix things which do not mix". To move on into a new relationship when there is emotional and physical fall-out from a previous marriage is adulterous in that the (probably negative) feelings for and about the ex-lover are taken into the new relationship. These feelings will have their impact on the new partner too, who may feel that the ex-husband or wife is an unwelcome part of the new relationship, and may have to deal with the fall-out.

The healing arts teach that it takes seven years for a human being's Chakras (emotional nerve-centres in the aura) to disconnect fully from an emotional and sexual relationship such as marriage. This process can be assisted through counselling, healing or other therapy but the principle is interesting. Jesus is saying a simple truth – that to move on to another relationship when there is emotional fall-out from a previous one, makes adulterers of us. Anyone who has moaned about their ex-partner or thought "you're just the same as he/she was!" about a new one is carrying baggage from the previous relationship. Only when there is closure on an old relationship can a new one be started without adultery.

Any divorced person can see the sense behind Jesus' teaching at this level. Given the lack of availability of counselling and therapy in Jesus' day – and the short life-expectancy of people – it is very likely that a marriage break-up (which in those days was far more serious for the woman than for the man) would lead to un-resolvable emotional issues. I think that it is a valid modern interpretation that re-marriage is not a forbidden thing, only that it must be undertaken with great care and only when closure is achieved on a previous relationship. So often we jump from one lover to another – and a new relationship has very little chance of surviving under such pressure.

Mark's teaching on divorce is significantly different:

"And the Pharisees came to him, and asked him, 'Is it lawful for a man to put away his wife?' tempting him. And he answered and said unto them, 'What did Moses command you?'

And they said, 'Moses suffered to write a bill of divorcement, and to put her away.' And Jesus answered and said unto them, 'For the hardness of your heart he wrote you this precept. But from the beginning of the creation God made them male and female.

For this cause shall a man leave his father and mother, and cleave to his wife; and they twain shall be one flesh: so then they are no more twain, but one flesh.

What therefore God hath joined together, let not man put asunder.'

And in the house his disciples asked him again of the same. And he saith unto them, 'Whosoever shall put away his wife, and marry another, committeth adultery against her. And if a woman shall put away her husband, and be married to another, she committeth adultery.'" (Mark 10:1)

To start with, a woman *could not* put away her husband and be married to another in the Jewish world. She could leave her husband and she could instigate a divorce on many grounds, but any re-marriage on her part completely depended on the husband's willingness to give her the bill of divorcement. Even nowadays, an orthodox Jewish woman cannot remarry in the eyes of her faith if her ex-husband does not agree to a *get*. So Jesus, here, cannot be talking about legal divorce. Therefore, he must be referring to psychological divorce.

This section, from Mark, includes the original of the passage used in the Protestant wedding service: "Those whom God hath joined together, let no man put asunder."

This has two meanings – firstly that there is a spiritual level to true marriage. The vast majority of relationships have nothing to do with God or Spirit but are contracted for love or social reasons. These couples are *not* brought together by God, therefore they are not the marriages referred to here.

In a relationship that is consciously contracted at a spiritual level, there is a different level of agreement between the couple – and their marriage is sacred to their spiritual development. Such marriages, should they fail, can – and are – put asunder by God. I have seen examples in couples where one has continued commitment to his or her development and spiritual service and the other has turned away from the original course of the marriage. Where prayer and the intent for Divine Order have been invoked in the marriage, often, there is a sudden development that breaks the couple up. It would be adulterous for such a couple to stay together.

Mark also speaks of "hardness of heart" and this is a powerful statement, probably even more relevant to us today than it was in those days. We marry wearing rose-tinted spectacles, believing in the romance of the movies and when the hard times come, are not prepared to ride the difficulties and keep our hearts focused on what is good in the relationship.

Interestingly, in the twenty first century, where women have more freedom to make partnership decisions than ever before, heart disease (the hardening of arteries) has become far more common in women. Until the twentieth century it was considered a predominantly male disease but the modern woman competing in the corporate world is trained to harden her heart.

Luke's teaching is short and to the point (16:18): "Whosoever putteth away his wife, and marrieth another, committeth adultery; and whosoever marrieth her that is put away from her husband committeth adultery." Neither the psychological Mark nor the spiritual Luke add the rider "save for fornication" as the physical Matthew does. Interestingly the word used for fornication is *porneia* which can mean adultery with another adult of the opposite sex, but equally means homosexuality, incest, intercourse with animals *or* the worship of idols. Few marriages can survive any of those revelations about a spouse and those that do, are either a sham for social convenience – or evidence of psychological and spiritual growth of immense stature.

Luke also adds this intriguing rider:

"The children of this world marry, and are given in marriage: But they which shall be accounted worthy to obtain that world, and the resurrection from the dead, neither marry, nor are given in marriage: Neither can they die any more: for they are equal unto the angels; and are the children of God." (Luke 20:34)

This is understandably taken to mean that marriage is not a good idea for those in spiritual work or ministry, but again remember that the Greek words "to marry" or to be "given in marriage" refer back to the social contract of marriage rather than a mutual commitment made to God. An equally accurate translation of the passage for the mystic would be: "The children of life are given and taken in marriage. But those who strive to master eternity and to rise from spiritual lack (death) are neither given nor taken in marriage." In the Old Testament, many references are made to the "Children of Israel" and the "House of Israel" to differentiate between people who have not begun spiritual self-development and those who have (the Hebrew word Israel means "one who struggles with God").

If what Jesus is saying is an injunction against marriage for the spiritual seeker, then it is most unlikely that the relationship he had with Mary Magdalene would have been marriage *unless* he is referring to the spiritual seeker marrying someone who is not themselves a person of faith. That, certainly, is not helpful to the seeker's path. However, the text could also be seen as referring to those who are no longer incarnate and who are already in the spiritual world.

Divorce is not mentioned at all in the Gospel of John but it is the only Gospel that contains the story of the marriage at Cana (John 2:1). At the Divine level – which is beyond physical reality – the Earthly contract of marriage does not exist; instead we have the concept of the Sacred Marriage between ourselves and God. This can also be the relationship of two people, perhaps of opposite sexes, which is not sexual but is devoted to spiritual work. This is the most likely scenario between Jesus and Mary Magdalene and it was certainly the case between St Theresa of Avila and St John of the Cross and perhaps also between St Frances and St Clare of Assisi.

The marriage at Cana is a superb story of the meaning of Sacred Marriage. It is the first miracle: the turning of water into wine. It is notable for the working together of two people who understand the higher worlds of miracles and the passing of authority from Mary to Jesus. The son is reluctant to begin his work but his mother's confidence in him is both authoritative and empowering. Once he accepts his mission of working from the Divine level and raises his consciousness, a miracle is automatic. For the Church, this marriage feast is symbolic of the wedding of Christ with humanity. It is an example of two souls working together to serve a higher purpose. In this case it is Mary and Jesus. And it is this pairing which is still the driving force throughout the Roman Catholic world.

CHAPTER NINE

CELIBACY, ITS PURPOSE AND
WEAKNESS IN SPIRITUAL LIFE

For Yeshua, the time spent alone in prayer and contemplation after Tamar's and Sarah's deaths was both terrible and glorious. Apart from the world of family, away from the conventions of synagogue and Temple, he could unravel layer after layer of illusion, pain and doubt.

For the first days of his journey towards Jordan, he was still too confused to see the world of abundance around him, hardly noticing that when he needed water, he found it; when he required food, it was there. He had always known that passing holy men were fed by farmers and homesteaders and, as a child, he himself had often taken out offerings of bread, cheese and fruit to place on fig leaves in the crook of an olive tree on the road that passed by Nazareth. He had thought it a delightful custom; Simon and Yacob thought it a waste. "It will only be eaten by animals," they said. But their father was firm. "And so what if it is?" he said. "It is an offering to the Lord to do with as He will. It will feed the passing man, angel, bird or beast. The point is to give without expecting an outcome."

The other boys thought that silly but Yeshua and Yuda liked the practice and it became one of their regular routines. Mary and Salome often wanted to carry the food too, but they would be tempted to feed the birds and goats along the way and, anyway, the boys thought their sisters silly and soft. It was the sight of a mother and baby Oryx bursting through a grove of carob trees that brought memory flooding back.

He saw, clearly as if it were happening that very day, eight-year-old Salome holding out bread to a young Oryx, totally absorbed in its beauty while a leopard crouched, hidden in a grove of mustard and oleander, waiting to pounce. In those days, lion, leopard, cheetah and bear were still common in the hills of the Galilee and shepherds had to be both brave and observant to preserve their flock.

He was twelve; fast enough on his feet to get to his sister and to frighten the animal. His shouts shocked the little girl so she lost her balance and fell. The leopard hesitated, then backed away, wary of the boy's noise and waving arms. The Oryx bounded off and Salome, horribly shocked, burst into tears. Yeshua picked her up and held her in his arms, turning her face towards him so she would not see the leopard leap, race and catch the Oryx in one, smooth movement. Part of him wondered why he kept the sight from her; she had to grow up, had to know about life and death and the survival of the fittest, but he also knew that her innocence was precious. There would be enough blood later on.

This time though he saw no pursuing beast; perhaps his presence had scared it; perhaps it was a false alarm. But the experience opened his eyes and he looked around him at the abundance of life and glory around him. He was nearly half-way between Nazareth and Bethsaida, walking on paths made by goats and sheep driven by the local shepherds. The landscape was filled with trees and bushes all budding as the spring season was born and, if he paused and breathed deeply, he could just catch a trace of the honeyed scent of the beautiful white and pink almond blossoms on the hillsides to his left.

Something told him to observe and remember. He did not know yet that there were so few years left of his life on Earth or how incredible would be the demands on his time and energy; that it might be the last time of complete leisure, of being free. Below his feet, cyclamen, yellow daisies and red anemones peeped out from the newly sprouting grasses and in every direction he looked there were trees and plants that offered food or medicine: olive, fig, carob, mustard, mint, pistachio, date, wheat, barley. Galilee was bursting with the energy of spring.

Looking up, he saw the distant snows on the crown of Mount Hermon and above that the vast, clear and endless sky and the sun blazing over all Israel. A kite – or was it an eagle? – soared high overhead; calls of birds entered his consciousness, calling his attention back towards the ground. A flock of goldfinches was dipping and diving between olive trees and a robin's clear voice rang out from the heart of a carob bush.

All day he remained in that one spot, almost breathless with the beauty and the wonder of it. He watched bees, ants and beetles in the dry dust, felt the velvet and silk of the flower petals, marvelled at the color of their stamens and laughed as yellow pollen stained his fingertips.

He saw a pair of storks searching for a place to build their nest and the courtship of two wrens. Below him, on a better-used path, a goatherd and his charges wandered by, the animals taking their time and grazing their way with bells clanking. The boy's tuneless whistle caused the birds to cock their heads on one side in wonder and flutter farther away for safety. Then a young couple, the girl pregnant and sitting on the back of a small donkey, the young man slightly anxious and nagging at the beast to walk faster, passed along the pathway.

Yeshua watched it all, seeing the interweaving of life, the pattern of the seasons and feeling the joy of being a part of it all. The goatherd reminded him of his son, the young couple of himself and Tamar, the goldfinches of Sarah, the wrens of his mother. He thought long and hard about his father, Yosef, who had guided him and taught him the value of faith and strength. Now, he could feel the grief as a part of the joy; knowing what he heard, saw, smelled and felt on this day could only be so wonderful having known the life he had lived. At one time, tears coursed down his cheeks but he hardly knew if they came from grief or wonder. At another, a roe deer and her calf walked by, so close he could have reached out and touched them. The baby looked him in the eyes with pure trust and the mother did not swerve on her path.

"I am so grateful," he said at last, causing a grey dove to fly, wings clattering as she rose into the air in surprise at the unexpected voice. "I am so glad to be a part of this. We are all treasures held close to one heart; none greater, none lesser. Whatever is to come, I will always have

this understanding."

He was to need it in the three years left to him. He had direct contact with the Divine; every sight he saw, every sound he heard, every word he spoke, every scent he inhaled, every texture he felt was experienced by his God-self and his human self simultaneously; he knew of no difference between the two. And wherever he went there was a companionship with people, the land or animals, whenever he stopped and turned to look for them. And in his heart and mind there were memories to comfort and to remind him when his teaching grew too intellectual or too fierce. Then he would see the faces of Tamar, Sarah, Judith, Yosef, Miriam, Susannah and even Leah looking back at him, their stories living in his mind so that he could temper judgement with mercy, wisdom with understanding.

The disciples did not understand his willingness to allow women to join them along the way; they thought it was a weakness in him until he allowed his eyes to flash anger and his tongue to cut their traditional, unthought-through remarks to shreds. Once he had disciples, he was no longer Yeshua the carpenter but Jesus of Nazareth; no longer the husband, father, brother and kin of many but a teacher of souls. No matter how he loved them – Peter, Andrew, John, even his earthly brother Yacob when he joined them – he could not be fully their companion nor they his; he was too close to the Lord and they could not fully understand him. The relationship with the Divine was all-embracing, filled with mystery and delight but also with awe and, at its heart, a deep loneliness for someone who could truly share his thoughts, beliefs and knowledge.

The disciples, male and female, had each other. They could talk and argue and rest with each other but, to them, he was special and different. They loved and respected him; came to him if they were afraid or confused; but they were not his equals in faith or knowledge.

He wondered often if God were lonely too. Misunderstood, misinterpreted and derided by most. Of course that was a ridiculous thought; God was All, everything and complete but if we, on Earth, reflect the Divine back with our every thought, he considered, perhaps our loneliness is felt above as well.

Spiritual or physical passion

To walk the Earth without an equal is to be alone no matter how surrounded you are by others. It meant that Jesus could think uniquely; meditate deeply, communicate fully with God and the angels whenever he was alone and had given himself the time to do it. But when he was immersed in the crowds or teaching the men or women who surrounded him more and more as each day went past, there was no one to whom he could confide his human heart; his fears and his everyday wonder at what was happening to him. There was no one with whom he could discuss the day with thoughts shared without words and where there was a gentle hand to hold his and offer support, belief and comfort.

Religious ecstasy is quite as powerfully blissful as sexual orgasm and it comes with the advantage of automatically equal joy for your Divine partner. It also comes without any need for compiling joint Christmas card lists; worrying if your spouse is in debt or the need to take out the trash (physically, at least).

So there are advantages to celibacy as well as the obvious disadvantages. For the majority of the under 40s in the twenty first century where sexuality is the prime mover of nearly all advertising, the idea of living forever, or even for a specified time, without sex is challenging to say the least. But we forget how many long-lasting marriages are lived in quiet, unheralded celibacy for whatever reason and which still survive and maybe even thrive. The sexual urge may be very powerful but it is also very much a part of our nature-soul rather than our spiritual essence. A celibate life, lived with passion, may be far more fulfilling than a marriage where the spark has died.

Vestal Virgins

For women, in particular, celibacy has conferred power for centuries – and not just in Christianity. Vestal Virgins, the priestesses of the Roman

Goddess of the hearth and fire, were all celibate and they had more power and influence than any other women in Rome. It's logical to say that, given the fact that there were a maximum of six of them at any one time, they didn't affect society's attitude to women and celibacy much, but their image was incredibly powerful and even today most people know the appellation "Vestal Virgin".

A chosen virgin, aged between six and ten, had her hair shorn and from that moment was under the protection of the Goddess rather than her family. Unlike most Roman women, she was not subject to the *pater potestas* – the father's right of life or death over his daughter – and could own her own property, make a will and vote. She had one other amazing power, which was to nullify a sentence of death on any criminal met accidentally in the street. However, anyone who pushed to see or speak to her risked the death penalty.

The Vestals were required to take three vows. The first was allegiance to the Goddess Vesta; the second was to keep the Temple's flame constantly alight; the third vow was of chastity – emulating the goddess herself. If a Vestal Virgin broke this vow, punishment was severe – she was killed by being buried alive in a small underground room where she had room to move, some light and food. It was ruled that a body that had been consecrated to sacred service could not be allowed to starve to death. So, the transgressor presumably just waited until the air ran out. Roman records show that just eighteen of the Vestal Virgins across nine centuries took lovers and suffered this horrible fate. The others either got away with it or counted love well lost in return for service to the Goddess and, quite possibly, for power.

The vows of the Vestal Virgins were not taken for life, but for 30 years. For the first ten they were students, the second ten they tended the flame as priestesses and for the last ten they trained their successors. At the end of their time in service, aged between 36 and 40 they were free to marry. Very few indeed are on record as having taken up this opportunity, maybe because they held their long-held rights as more valuable than a sexual relationship. For a man, marrying a former Vestal Virgin was highly prestigious; for the woman it would have been a strange experience indeed.

No one has ever recorded whether the Vestals were lonely. They had the company of five peers and despite the normal bickering between colleagues, they were all at the same level; they had the same goals. But were they true companions? Could they share hopes and fears, and trust in each other's kindness? What we do know is that being alone is not the only source of loneliness. Many people are bitterly lonely in a bad marriage and many who have been widowed or divorced would never even consider risking another bad bargain.

Early Christianity was a welcome refuge for widows in the Roman world who could "take the veil" of Christ and claim a religious privilege to avoid the Roman requirement for re-marriage for any woman of still reproductive age. Later on, nuns, particularly Prioresses and Abbesses, carried great influence in society, and still do in Catholic countries. Many an ex-Catholic school pupil can attest to the power of even the lowliest nun. Even though they had taken a vow of poverty, in the Middle Ages senior nuns and monks often represented great wealth within their convent or monastery. Until Henry VIII of England's dissolution of the monasteries in 1538, a great many of the ecclesiastical centres were incredibly wealthy – and many were also corrupt both financially and sexually.

There is a common belief that ancient Rome was rife with homosexuality but in fact bisexuality was far more the norm. Aristocratic Roman men had the right to have sex with their male slaves – the penetrative act being acceptable while being penetrated was seen as being effeminate – but openly homosexual relationships between men were rare and all men were expected to marry and have children. So the lamentable incidents of Catholic priests and young boys that are reported in the press nowadays are little different from the activities of powerful men in ancient Rome. However, openly homosexual relationships between priests is a much more modern phenomenon.

A celibate church

The word celibacy from the Latin *caelebs*, meaning unmarried, used to mean just that. Given that pre-marital sex was common in ancient Rome, particularly before the Augustinian laws on marriage, you could be a fully sexually active celibate. However, over the centuries the word has come to mean someone who has renounced sex and marriage, especially for religious purposes.

Celibacy was not actually required of Catholic priests until the late Middle Ages, although it has been practised voluntarily for 2000 years. Religious groups have included celibates since the principle of withdrawing from the secular world began (the Alexandrian Therapeutae are a good example). Judaism has always frowned upon celibacy as it banishes the hope of begetting the Messiah. The Essenes embraced it, but only for an inner core of men. Jesus did not prescribe it although he did say that marriage was not for everyone. His famous speech about eunuchs has been used to justify many forms of celibacy.

What he is reported to have said is:

"For there are some eunuchs, which were so born from their mother's womb: and there are some eunuchs, which were made eunuchs of men: and there be eunuchs, which have made themselves eunuchs for the kingdom of heaven's sake. He that is able to receive it, let him receive it." (Matthew 19:12).

The word eunuch has several meanings. It is the guard of a woman's bed-chamber; a man who cannot have children for natural reasons or who has been physically castrated; or a man who abstains from marriage for any reason whatsoever, religious or not. As the saying follows directly from the disciples' comments that marriage was more difficult than they thought, it is perfectly fair to say that Jesus is replying that some people simply cannot or do not want to be husbands or wives. He is not saying that marriage is wrong; simply that it is challenging. He is also not talking about homosexuality, although it is perfectly understandable, given the bad rap that all forms of homosexuality are given in the Old Testament, for gay people to want some kind of benediction.

Jesus says nothing against homosexuality in any of the Gospels. Both men and women who do not feel the natural sexual urges of the average human often find themselves called to the spiritual life but, if they are withdrawn from the world that the rest of us live in, how can they empathise with our worldly problems? The answer given, of course, is that they are inspired by God and that may well be so. But the urge for celibacy is not common among humanity; sexual drives are natural and powerful. So, apart from the desire by Roman widows not to marry a second time, why did celibacy become so essential a part of the early Roman Church?

We are told that the first Christians were inspired by Jesus' example and St Paul praised virginity as being better than marriage (1 Corinthians 7) but Paul also made it very clear that he had no instruction from Christ concerning celibacy and all the views he gave were his own. Virtues of self-control, self-denial and the freedom from family cares which would leave more time for prayer, contemplation and apostolic activity were certainly praised throughout the early church, but that's not all the story.

It's very important here to look at the context in which any of the New Testament teachings about marriage are couched. In a nutshell, they believed that the end of the world was nigh. Whether or not Jesus himself actually believed during his lifetime that "the end times" were coming, the words attributed to him imply that something like that was thought to be in the wind, if not immediately:

"When you hear of wars and revolutions, do not be frightened. These things must happen first but the end will not come right away." (Luke 21:9). A decade after the crucifixion, however, the end of the world was being prophesied in a big way – and it was coming sooner rather than later. The early Christians genuinely believed that Jesus would come again in their lifetime and then the Day of Judgement would follow: "But the end of all things is at hand: be ye therefore sober, and watch unto prayer." (1 Peter 7:7).

Paul himself wrote:

"For the Lord himself shall descend from heaven with a shout, with the voice of the archangel, and the trump of God: and the dead in Christ shall rise first. Then we which are alive and remain shall be caught up together with them in the clouds to meet the Lord in the air: and so shall we ever be with the Lord." (Thessalonians 1:4)

Later, he urges readers of this letter to be alert at all times, because the second coming and the end would happen within their lifetimes. When the Christian Thessalonicans were persecuted by the Roman Empire, they, quite understandably, believed the end had begun.

So, all Paul's teachings on marriage and celibacy have to be interpreted with that view in mind. To marry – and to beget children – when the end of the world was nigh was a bad idea; it could only cause pain especially if the partner were not a believer and was going to be taken away to hell on the Day of Judgement. So, this exciting new celibate option of "brothers and sisters in Christ" was not expected to be a long-term thing.

"Yet those who are married will experience distress in this life and I would spare you. I mean, brothers and sisters, the appointed time has grown short... For the present form of this world is passing away," says Paul in 1 Corinthians 7:28. Often this section is translated without the rider about the end of the world, which makes it look simply as if being married meant trouble. The translation above is from the Revised Standard Bible – the King James says:

"But and if thou marry, thou hast not sinned; and if a virgin marry, she hath not sinned. Nevertheless such shall have trouble in the flesh: but I spare you. But this I say, brethren, the time is short: it remaineth, that both they that have wives be as though they had none."

As with everything Biblical, it's all in the translation. But the context is clearly there for those who look for it. Paul is often lambasted for his attitudes towards women but, again, within the context of the times, he was not as bad as many think. For example, his injunction to women to cover their heads and not to prophesy in the streets was given at a time when the cult of Cybele or Magna Mater (Great Mother) was at its height in Rome. The great goddess' priests were called the *galli* – they were self-castrated, wore women's clothes, shaved their bodies and had long hair. They were viewed with horror by many in Rome, particularly during their parades and feast times, when they danced in the streets and shed their own blood. At their major festival in March they mourned the death of the Goddess' son Attis and then danced with joy at his resurrection. To the uninitiated, this was very similar to the Christian story of a holy child, death and resurrection. Any Christian long-haired, feminine creatures who started proclaiming death and resurrection in the streets might well be mistaken for priests of Cybele and that, the early Christians could not afford.

Women were a very useful part of the new Christian community; they provided homes where the travelling preachers could stay and these rapidly became recognised centres of the new faith. Also, many wealthy, independent widows were more than generous financially to any group that assisted them in avoiding the trials of re-marriage.

Despite the fact that the end of the world did not come, the cult of celibacy endured. It had already attracted those to whom the idea appealed – and they were the ones in charge. However, no strict law of celibacy existed in the first three centuries of Christianity even though the idea was honored by members of the new church's clergy who probably wanted to disassociate themselves from every other available religion.

Tertullian admired the number of celibate clergy and Origen made a distinct contrast between the "carnal paternity" of the Levite priests and the "spiritual fatherhood" of the New Testament Priests. Clement of Alexandria, however, approved publicly of priests who were married – as long as they intended to have children. St John Chrysostom wrote texts that said a bishop should have a wife. This interpretation was revived in the sixteenth century by protestant reformers.

The first time that an actual law of celibacy was proposed was at the Ecumenical Council of Nicea in 325 CE. Paphuntius, a celibate Egyptian bishop, opposed it strongly saying that the ancient tradition that opposed marriage after ordination to the priesthood should remain but that there should be no bar to ordination after marriage. The Council agreed – and added a rider that clergymen should not have any unmarried women in their homes who were not near relatives, in order to remove any temptation.

The idea of clerical celibacy developed during and after the fourth century although its practice was far more stringent in the West than the East. The Eastern Church's Council of Ancyra in 314 CE allowed a candidate for the deaconate to choose between celibacy or marriage and bound him to keep that decision. A few years later the Council of Gangra condemned any disdain for married priests within the Church. Bishops however, practised what's known as "continence" within marriage and this custom passed into Church law at the Council of Trullo in 692 CE. From then on, a man could only be raised to Bishop if his wife agreed to retire to a monastery. Ordained priests, deacons and sub-deacons could not marry but they were free to keep wives married before ordination. This law has remained the same since then – but the true practice is only to ordain unmarried priests to the level of Bishop.

In the Latin Church the pattern was similar. At what was really a provincial local Council of Elvira in Grenada in or about the year 300 CE, bishops, priests and deacons in that area were prescribed continence (sexual abstention) and, although no further legislation was passed for a further 86 years, the Pope Siricus made it a universal practice in the Roman Church. Councils in Carthage in 309 and 402 CE prohibited matrimonial intercourse for deacons and priests, and so it went on with ruling after ruling.

The wives of clergy were treated as sisters and were actually called deaconess, priestess or episcopes. The wife of a priest or deacon remained mistress of his house, but the wife of a bishop had to live in a separate home or retire to a convent.

However, the proximity of man and woman (who were, presumably, fond enough of each other to marry) continued to cause problems and by the eighth century, violations of the law were known to be commonplace. Partly this was due to more and more people joining the clergy because the pay was good rather than through vocation.

The observance of the rules varied according to which Pope, Emperor or State was the most powerful until, by the tenth century, married priests were more common than not. Finally, the first and second Ecumenical Councils of the Lateran (1123 and 1139) removed the possibility of clerical marriage after ordination to the lowest state of sub-deacon by making this and any other higher orders a lawful impediment to marriage.

From then on, despite debates and blips, this was the state of the world – you could just about be married but you couldn't have sex.

Finally, in 1918, the Code of Canon Law prohibited marriage at all without special Papal dispensation. Such dispensations were given to dissenting priests who transferred to the Church of Rome after the beginning of ordination of women in the Anglican Church in the USA in 1974. It is difficult to separate out the religious view that a celibate life is better than a married one for those in holy orders, because of the strong line of misogyny that has developed from many religious texts over the last 2000 years.

Companionship

For the mystic, it is fairly easy to distinguish between the diatribes against women per se and the definitions of basic masculine and feminine principles. Kabbalah teaches that pure masculinity is as out of balance as pure femininity and that equilibrium is required between the two. All men have a feminine side as all women have a masculine side; the priority is to create a balance within the self. Where there is a physical marriage this balance also has to be worked out between the couple (whether or not they are of opposite sexes) and this is often the cause of much marital discord.

From study, experience and observation, I would surmise that living a life of devotion to spirit is much easier as a single person than it is as part of a couple. The only exceptions to this would be a relationship where both parties were equally committed to their spiritual growth or where one was totally supportive of the other's quest.

Many of the companions with whom I have worked have complained of the impossibility of morning meditation or ritual when there is a partner or a family to engage with in the morning. Some do wake earlier than the rest of their family but, even so, such discipline is difficult to maintain at times of family sickness or holidays. And a spouse may resent never having their loved one with them when they, themselves, wake.

Those who are truly committed to a spiritual path do find the time – even two minutes of prayer or meditation are infinitely more value than none at all – but without the outside support and guidance of companions on the same path it is only a saint who can significantly advance their spiritual growth when there are children to nurture and deadlines to meet.

The issue of companions is one of the reasons why the monastic life was so successful for many generations – and continued to be so in Europe even after the dissolution of the monasteries in England. So celibacy is good for the spiritual path as long as there are equals with whom to share your religious life. Religious hermits are very rare and frequently have psychological issues which make it impossible for them and for others to live comfortably together. Another reason for the success of monastic life was that the life of a religious in olden days meant comparative comfort; food might be basic in the communities committed to poverty but it was always provided. Likewise medical care and spiritual and personal guidance. Not to mention hard work and routine to keep the mind focused. For those in the wealthier orders or higher up the pecking order there was also the lure of education. Women in convents had the opportunity to read, write and study, and to become artists of calligraphy as well as musicians, herbalists and farmers. Yes, nuns had to have a man present in order to celebrate Mass but in all other respects they had autonomy over their own lives.

That said, it is not easy to live in a community of your own sex where the habits of others may be a constant source of irritation, but it is equally not much worse than an unhappy marriage with a partner demanding sex and the constant addition of children who would be loved but who can barely be afforded.

For centuries, men and women would be placed in monasteries with or without their consent but nowadays very few people embrace a religious life involuntarily. Therefore, celibacy is a choice that can be made with due consideration. Even so, companionship is necessary; spiritual work is rarely comfortable and never convenient and the support of ones' peers is essential for the inner strength required in difficult times.

For those teachers who have risen above their peers and who are always expected to lead rather than to lean on others, the price of leadership is high. A deep, abiding, loving relationship with God *can* fill all the gaps. But a companion soul to smile at you in the physical world is a pearl of great price.

CHAPTER TEN

MARY MAGDALENE, WOMAN OF SUBSTANCE

The market traders in Magdala were always pleased to see the lady wander aimlessly up from the ornate white house by the harbour. Often, should they be able to catch her attention – for she was usually lost in some inner world – she bought their wares simply for the sake of something to do. She had servants to buy and cook her food for her and to make her clothes, so all she could purchase herself were fripperies. Those she would buy at too high a price because she could not be bothered to haggle. Why should she? She had more money than she knew what to do with and a business that brought more in every day.

Her father, Laban the fish-processor, had been the wealthiest man in the region; his was the only place for miles where you could take the catch that you could not sell on the morning you had caught them. It was his workers who smoked, salted and pickled the fish so they could be carried all over Galilee for families who had never seen the sea to buy, eat and enjoy.

The fish-processor's only child had been married well; to the son of a priest in the Temple of Jerusalem, although the crueller gossips wondered if he would be able to handle the stink of fish on her hands and in her robes once he had looked beyond her obvious beauty. Miriam was statuesque and clear-eyed with unblemished skin, but she was wilful and had been ill-raised in the religion of her birth.

In Magdala, Roman and Egyptian gods held as much sway as the Jewish Deity and for those busy in the world of merchandise it did not pay to be too nice in your practices and beliefs; after all, business was business. Being married to the son of a priest must have come as a shock to a girl as used to offering a sacrifice to Artemis or Isis as going to the Temple for the holy festivals.

So no one was particularly surprised when she returned to Magdala 10 years later. Of course, she could have been widowed but the word of her divorce spread like wildfire before her. She had been apart from her husband too often since her father died for her marriage to have been a success. Her son was to stay with her husband, Aaron, and there had been no dispute about her dowry. Aaron had never taken any interest in fish processing; he had ambition within the Temple. Miriam had, after all, not turned out suitable; initially she had produced the correct sex of child, but when no more sons or daughters arrived, her boredom – and what they called disruptive tendencies – were not popular in the higher echelons of Jerusalem's society. She would never be an aristocrat and it was irritating for all that she was wealthier than any of them. Of course, the wealth all belonged to her husband while they were married, but Miriam still travelled back to Magdala every month to oversee the family business; Miriam the practical and business-like woman. And whose hands still smelt of fish.

Miriam was not pleased when her son returned to Magdala on his marriage, claiming his share of the business. Timon had no flair for the priesthood but he knew a good money-spinner when he saw it and he chose wealth over the aristocrat's aversion to trade. He did not approve of his mother; she had been divorced after all. She had to see sense that he was the rightful heir to her fish business and he should be acknowledged – and paid – as that. His wife, Joanna, produced children at the drop of a hat and enjoyed her life as a wealthy woman in Magdala, although she constantly spoke of how much better a town Jerusalem was. Mother and daughter-in-law did not get on. Miriam was not an adoring grandmother and her stern ways with Joanna's adored children placed an even stronger bar between mother and son than before.

He wanted her to hand over the business to them, but she knew he was lazy at heart, as well as greedy, and he would not take care of the equipment or the servants.

"This is a good business; it should be run well," she would say, rolling up her sleeves and working with the servants in order to check that everything was correct. That was beyond eccentric to Timon and Joanna and spoke of her common stock. They would not go home stinking of fish at the end of the day.

So, Miriam was resentful, unhappy and unfulfilled. On this day, she felt particularly depressed. She stopped by the little synagogue where her father and mother had taken her when she was a child and, on a whim, stepped in. There was a group of men in there, praying. She sat silently at the side behind the curtain where the women sat and listened. She did not realise that she was sighing loudly and when the curtain was switched open by the caretaker, she glared at him defensively.

"You are not welcome here," he said. "Go. You have not paid a subscription and you have no man to pray for you. Be gone!"

Miriam opened her mouth to berate him but depression settled on her. What was the point? They were all the same, priests, rabbis, whoever. Even the priestesses of Artemis were arrogant and none of them truly cared for their congregations. She got up and left without a word and walked back down towards the harbour and then along the coastal path towards Dalmanutha. The day stretched before her long and tedious.

A group of children ran past, filled with the brightness of excitement and youth. "Come and see the prophet!" one of them called out to a friend. "He's down at the shore. He's quite mad!"

There was nothing else to do. Miriam followed the group through the village to the sea; quite a crowd was gathering in the harbour but she was tall – and not averse to pushing her way through the other people.

On the harbour's edge, a man was sitting, looking both patient and intense. You could tell that he was trying to speak but could not get a word out and, once Miriam was close enough to hear, she could tell why. A group of Magdala's Pharisees were gathered around him, their blue and white striped robes billowing in the sea breeze. They were questioning *him on aspects of the Law; the Pharisees words were tumbling out, more in the wish to impress those listening with their knowledge and erudition than in a desire to hear the prophet's answer. They were so busy debating among themselves that they weren't giving him any space to answer. For a moment she thought she saw a twitch of amusement at the corner of his mouth but it was gone before she could be sure.*

Was he a prophet? Miriam looked at him long and hard, deciding. He was no scruffier than the average man; his two companions were obviously fishermen but his robes were too long. His face, observed closely, looked older than she had thought and there were traces of tiredness in the lines of his brow and the set of his mouth, but even so there was a light within his eyes that drew her. Somehow she knew that he had suffered but that he had weathered that suffering and did not hold it with pain any more. A spark of interest ran through her and she lifted her powerful voice and shouted: "Let the prophet speak!"

There was silence; everyone turned and looked at her but Miriam did not care. Because he looked at her too and his gaze took in everything from her body to her soul. And for the first time, she felt her spirit stir. An always longed-for, never experienced lift arose inside her heart. It was not love; not desire; it was what she had always missed and never known before. Her heart plummeted as he looked away; the Pharisees starting their diatribes again and the crowd, having assessed her, negated her and turned back to the show.

Then he spoke. It should have been hard to hear his voice in the melee but the words were clear and it seemed as though he was speaking directly to her: "I call heaven and earth to bear witness unto you this day that I have set before you life and death; blessing and cursing. Therefore I say unto you 'choose life, that you and what you sow may live.'" (Deuteronomy 30:19).

He stood up. "There is no point, they do not have the ability to listen," he said quietly to one of his friends. "I am tired; shall we go?"

"Yes Master," said the man, a burly dark fisherman. "Thomas and

Andrew are back and we are ready to sail."

"Then let's go," said the man, impervious to the Pharisees fury that he had drawn his attention from them – they were far from finished.

He bowed to them (with not a little irony) and turned away, walking almost directly onto a brightly-painted fishing boat that bobbed in the water with his weight. The two companions followed him and Miriam could see other men already waiting on the boat. The crowd made noises of disgust: no argument, no fight; what was the point? They began to disperse.

As the men untied the ropes and the boat began to move away, Miriam felt an impulse within her. She ran forward and called out, "Rabbi! Rabbi!"

He heard her and turned. "Well?"

The words came out of her mouth before she had thought: "Why did they throw me out of the synagogue today? I wanted to pray."

"Bitterness," he said in Hebrew, not the Aramaic that he had spoken earlier. "Your bitterness wears you through and through. It eats at you. Let it go. Sell your possessions and follow the truth. Follow the strong waters. It's your choice to possess the Kingdom of Heaven or to be possessed by the kingdom of Man."

"What shall I do?" she implored him, unable to take in his words at first but hearing her name spoken again and again in Hebrew: Mar – bitterness; Mara – disobedient; Meri – rebellious; Mara – strengthen; Marar-yam – strong sea.

"Change," he said and smiled at her. "Follow me."

Then he waved, turned away and walked to the brow of the boat as it moved out of earshot with the chop, chop, chop of the rowers and the waves.

She sat, suddenly, on the harbour wall, where he had sat. "Change," she said to herself. "Follow me." For a long while she sat there, slumped. It looked as though she was half asleep and several people passing looked at her askance. One or two who knew her spoke her name but she raised a hand to ward them off: her mind was racing. At last, she spoke. "Not Miriam," she said. "Not Bitterness, but Mary-am, Strong Waters. Mary. That's who I'll be. Mary the Strong."

That very afternoon she sought out the scribes who dealt with property exchange and put in motion her son's much desired take-over of the family firm. "Let go of the bitterness; let go of being possessed," she muttered to herself. "He can do what he likes with it."

Then, feeling free for the first time in years, she walked home and told her servants she was leaving on a long journey. Only one of them, her childhood friend Abigail, was willing to accompany her; two she retained to take care of the house and the rest were astonished – and displeased – to be given two months' notice.

"How did I ever need eight servants?" she asked herself, the fire within her building. "I must have been mad!"

"Not mad," said an inner voice. "Possessed."

Some said of her later that she gave up all she had but that was not quite true; she kept the land her mother had left to her and rented out her home so there was always income both for her and for all the disciples. She always had more than enough; a woman raised in such riches will only ever manifest more and, in any case, they all lived a simple life. Her purse was never empty and she was proud to be a means of support for her teacher when he needed it.

She caught up with him at Bethsaida and, together with Abigail, sat and listened. For six weeks she said nothing to him, but she knew he was aware of her. She learnt from the others of the death of his wife; she saw and learnt how he had come through that time and she began to lose her own anger through the wanting to be like him. When she did begin her questions it seemed like they would never end. But she hungered and thirsted for what he said and, unlike so many of the men, she understood him. Her soul drank his essence and, through it, made itself whole. She among all of them realised that he was showing a way, a path. He was not the goal but the signpost; not the destination but the journey.

The men, mostly, tolerated her; she did nothing wrong; did not encroach. Her joy was in knowing that she was home at last. She could let go the need to compete; to show off; to be the smart one. And, because of that, he would choose to sit with her by the fireside because he knew he could find rest there.

What we know about Mary Magdalene

Mary Magdalene has always been one of the most misunderstood – and reviled – women in religious history. She is still misinterpreted by those who wish her only well and who see her as the Holy Grail, the wife of Christ. Her relationship with Jesus has had to be downgraded into marriage in order that people can attempt to understand it. Obviously, if they had as special a relationship as the Gnostic Gospels of Philip and of Mary Magdalene suggest, they must have been lovers. Not at all.

Let's start with the famous *Da Vinci Code* claim that Leonardo Da Vinci painted Mary Magdalene sitting next to Jesus at the last supper. In the book, by Dan Brown, the hero, Robert Langdon, looks at the painting and has the stunning revelation that the image of St John is, in fact a woman. Yes, it certainly looks like a girl. And if this were the only painting where the apostle John looked a little effeminate, then he might have a point. Unfortunately, it is not.

Leonardo was not even a ground-breaker in painting an effeminate male in a painting about Jesus. He lived between the years of 1452 to 1519 but earlier, in the fourteenth century before he was even a dot of paint in his father's eye, Paul, Herman and Jean Limbourg, from Nijmegen in what is now known as the Netherlands, were painting Les Très Riches Heures – a magnificent Book of Hours for the Duke of Berry. One of the images from that work represents the healing of the possessed boy in Mark 9:17. The boy is full grown but a very androgenous figure with tumbling long dark curly hair and a feminine face and elegant hands. The only way you could tell he was male was his muscular legs.

Even more telling is the image of the Apostle John in the Flemish artist Juste the Gand's Last Supper, painted in 1474. John is beardless and wearing a feminine-style cape of entirely different style from that of all the other disciples. You could easily believe he was a girl. Some people say that Leonardo Da Vinci was gay. Certainly, in 1476 he and three others were anonymously accused of having sex with a beautiful boy model and male prostitute called Jacopo Saltarelli. The accusations were dropped without trial but, given that there is no trace of a woman in Leonardo's life and that there is evidence of a series of beautiful boy apprentices of apparently little artistic talent, homosexuality is an understandable assumption for a more tolerant modern world to make. However, in those times the devotion to classical Greek art and the beautiful young men depicted in ancient statues was extremely fashionable and Leonardo was not the only painter to be surrounded by young male muses.

One more effeminate John is to be found in Ford Maddox Brown's 1848 Pre-Raphaelite painting of Jesus washing the disciples' feet. John is blond and girly – and one of the other disciples has his arm around him in a protective hug.

So, lovely story though it is – and important as Mary Magdalene may have been – the idea that Leonardo is painting a woman holds very little water. What is so interesting is how many people want and need this modern legend to be true. There certainly is evidence that there might have been something special between Jesus and Mary, especially in the Nag Hammadi scrolls. These scrolls notably include the Gospels of Thomas, Philip and of Mary Magdalene herself.

So let's look at all the evidence we have about Mary Magdalene.

She is mentioned in all four Gospels and each one acknowledges that she was the first witness of the risen Christ (Mark is a bit doubtful here because scholars believe that the ending of the Gospel of Mark was tacked on a few years after the original was written). Mary Magdalene is named twelve times in the Gospels but only one is placed before the crucifixion (Luke 8:02). There is one at the cross (John 19:25) and there are ten after Jesus' death, including two mentions of Jesus having driven seven devils out of her (Mark 16:9 and Luke 8:1). Only three of the mentions also include another woman called Mary; probably Mary of Bethany but this is unproven. Those texts that write solely of Mary Magdalene are Mark 16:9 and John 20:1 and 20:18.

Apart from the fact that Mary Magdalene is the person charged with telling the disciples the news that Jesus has resurrected from the dead, I would say the most telling story about her comes in Luke:

"After this, Jesus traveled about from one town and village to another, proclaiming the good news of the kingdom of God. The Twelve were with him and also some women who had been cured of evil spirits and diseases: Mary (called Magdalene) from whom seven demons had come out; Joanna the wife of Cuza, the manager of Herod's household; Susanna; and many others. These women were helping to support them out of their own means."(Luke 8:1-3)

This is a distinct statement that Jesus' ministry was supported by wealthy women, one of whom was Mary Magdalene. Had she been his wife, her money would have belonged to him and this mention is unlikely to have been made. It is important to emphasise that the earliest available evidence shows women *did* have some part in Jesus' ministry as his followers.

One of the earliest of all original texts that is known today is the Dura-Europus scroll which dates back to the second century CE. This translation by D.C. Parker, D.G.K. Taylor and M.S. Goodacre (*Studies in the Early Text of the Gospels and Acts*, p. 201): "of [Zebed]ee and Salome a[nd] the women [amongst] those who followed him from [Galil]ee to see the cr[ucified one]." The sections in [ ] are missing but Salome and women "those who followed him" is clearly stated.

Probably the most common misunderstanding about Mary is the idea that she was the woman with the alabaster jar who anoints Jesus when he is at the house of Simon the Pharisee. The Gospels have four stories of the anointing of Jesus by a woman but none identify her with Mary Magdalene. In the earliest versions (Mark 14:3-9 and Matthew 26: 6-13) the unnamed woman is not identified as a sinner and she anoints Jesus' head (in those days this could be seen as an indication of Jesus' coming death). John (11:2) identifies the woman as Mary of Bethany and has her wiping Jesus' feet with her hair after anointing him.

Luke (7:36-50) tells the story much earlier in Jesus' life, saying that the unidentified woman is a repentant sinner who weeps, wipes Jesus' feet with her hair and anoints them with perfumed oil. He tells her that her faith has saved her which is slightly different from driving seven devils out of her. The idea of driving devils from someone was associated either with madness or severe sickness and this woman obviously had neither. Her actual sin is not identified; nowhere is there any indication that it is sexual in origin. All that libel came later.

The Gospel of Mary dates back to about 125 CE which makes it one of the oldest texts of the early Christian Church apart from the four Gospels themselves. It is part of what is known as the Berlin Codices and was not discovered with the 13 texts found at Nag Hammadi. It is often thought to be one of these because it is of similar date and origin and is referred to by scholars as being a part of the Nag Hammadi *Library*. In it, Mary Magdalene is clearly shown as having special understanding of Jesus in the often-quoted extract from chapter five: "Peter said to Mary, 'Sister, we know that the Saviour loved you more than the rest of women.'" But the rest of that chapter, which takes place after the resurrection, makes it clear that this is a spiritual relationship, not a physical one. It reads:

"....they were grieved. They wept greatly, saying, How shall we go to the Gentiles and preach the gospel of the Kingdom of the Son of Man? If they did not spare Him, how will they spare us?"

Then Mary stood up, greeted them all, and said to her brethren,

'Do not weep and do not grieve nor be irresolute, for His grace will be entirely with you and will protect you. But rather, let us praise His greatness, for He has prepared us and made us into Men.' When Mary said this, she turned their hearts to the Good, and they began to discuss the words of the Saviour.

Peter said to Mary, 'Sister we know that the Saviour loved you more than the rest of woman. Tell us the words of the Saviour which you remember which you know, but we do not, nor have we heard them.'

Mary answered and said, 'What is hidden from you I will proclaim to you.' And she began to speak to them these words: 'I, she said, I saw the Lord in a vision and I said to Him, Lord I saw you today in a vision.' He answered and said to me, 'Blessed are you that you did not waver at the sight of Me. For where the mind is there is the treasure.'

I said to Him, 'Lord, how does he who sees the vision see it, through the soul or through the spirit?'

The Saviour answered and said, 'He does not see through the soul nor through the spirit, but the mind that is between the two that is what sees the vision and it is ....'"

The rest of this chapter is missing.

Wife or prostitute?

The two phrases that cause all the excitement, particularly in *Holy Blood, Holy Grail* and *The Da Vinci Code,* come from the Gospel of Philip, which was found at Nag Hammadi. The first one is: "There were three who always walked with the Lord: Mary, his mother, and her sister, and Magdalene, the one who was called his companion."

The better-known quotation is:

"And the companion of the [...] Mary Magdalene. [...] loved her more than all the disciples, and used to kiss her often on her […] The rest of the disciples [...]. They said to him 'Why do you love her more than all of us?' The Saviour answered and said to them, 'Why do I not love you like her?'"

Many researchers and books have added in the word "mouth" for where Jesus placed his kisses. This is pure supposition.

And why, if Mary Magdalene is Jesus' wife, is anyone surprised that he should love her more, or kiss her? Surely they would be surprised if he did not. In Dan Brown's *Da Vinci Code*, Sir Leigh Teabing specifies the word "companion" to be the Aramaic "wife". As mentioned previously, the Gospel of Philip is written in Coptic, probably translated from Greek, and not in Aramaic and the author uses two different words for companion, one Greek – *koinonos* – and one Coptic – *hotre*. Neither is known to be used anywhere else in ancient texts to mean wife.

Koinonos appears in the New Testament seven times (Matthew 23:30, Luke 5:10, 1 Corinthians 10:18, 2 Corinthians 1:7, Hebrews 10.33, Philemon 1:17 and 2 Peter 1:4). Never once is it used except for man-to-man or human-to-Christ relationships. The word wife is a challenge in the New Testament because the word *gunay* is used both for woman and for wife. But in the King James Version it is used to mean wife 71 times in the New Testament and the only exception (1 Peter 3:7), is the use of the word *gunakeios* which means "belonging to the woman/wife/feminine". The word *koinonos* means fellowship or sharing with someone or in something ranging from friendship to business.

In the *Journal of Religion and Popular Culture* (Vol XII*)*, Dr Nancy Calvert-Koyzis of King's University College, University of Western Ontario, makes it clear that in the Gospel of Philip, when someone is spoken of as someone's wife, the Coptic word for wife is used rather than the Greek or Coptic for 'companion' (Gospel of Philip 70, 19; 76, 7; 82, 1). What is also apparent from the Nag Hammadi Library Gospels is that the disciple Peter did not like Mary or her influence. This is the Peter who became the foundation of the Roman Catholic Church.

From the Gospel of Mary: "Peter asked the others about the Saviour.

Did he really speak with a woman in private? Should we all listen to her? Did he really prefer her to us?" And: "Levi said to Peter, you are always angry. Now I see you are arguing against this woman like an adversary. If the Saviour made her worthy, who are you to reject her?"

From the Pistis Sophia (the most extensive Gnostic scripture known before the discovery of the Nag Hammadi scrolls, believed to have been written in the third century and preserved in what is known as the Codex Askewianus): "Mary came forward and said 'My Master, I understand that I can come forward at any time but I am afraid of Peter because he threatens me.'"

John Dominic Crossan, Professor Emeritus of Religious Studies at DePaul University, Chicago, and author of 20 books on the historical Jesus including *Jesus: A Revolutionary Biography*, *Who Killed Jesus* and *The Birth of Christianity* (HarperCollins) sums it up for me beautifully when he says: "They didn't attack Mary Magdalene because she was Mrs. Jesus. They attacked her because she was a major leader, that she was up there with Peter and the rest and they fought like hell to put her back down in her place."

So how did this woman, portrayed in so many Gospels, turn into a repentant prostitute? It didn't start out like that, according to early Church literature. The second century church father Hippolytus describes Mary and the other women disciples as Brides of Christ, faithful women who redeemed the disobedience of Eve. In his commentary on Solomon's "Song of Songs" in the third century, St Hippolytus even gives Mary Magdalene the title of "apostle to the apostles" and her star remained bright up until the fifth century when Ambrose, Bishop of Milan, also described Mary Magdalene as the New Eve clinging to Christ as a Tree of Life and redeeming the unfaithfulness of the first Eve. Other Church Fathers, Tertullian, Origen, Dionysius, Pseudo-Clement, Ambrose, Augustine and Gregory of Antioch were also strong in her praise.

It was only at the end of the sixth century that Mary Magdalene the prostitute hit the headlines. Pope Gregory I decided that it was too confusing to have so many different women in the Gospels, especially several called Mary, and ruled that several of the un-named mentions of women must be of Mary Magdalene. In an Easter sermon in 591 he is reported to have said, "She whom Luke calls the sinful woman, whom John calls Mary, we believe to be the Mary from whom seven devils were ejected according to Mark. And what did these seven devils signify, if not all the vices?"

The vices he was referring to were the seven cardinal (or deadly) sins as defined by – guess who? – Pope Gregory I himself. They are extravagance (later translated as lust), gluttony, greed, sloth (laziness), anger, envy and pride (also translated as vanity).

Pope Gregory's ruling was at best careless and at worst ignorant as the Gospel of John states clearly that the woman with the alabaster jar was Mary of Bethany not Mary Magdalene. Both appellations denoted the town of origin of the woman concerned and acted in the way that surnames do today.

Even so, Gregory did rehabilitate Mary in the same speech: "She turned the mass of her crimes to virtues, in order to serve God entirely in penance" (the seven holy virtues being chastity, temperance, charity, diligence, meekness, kindness and humility) but, even so, a legend was born.

However, the Eastern Christian Church tradition did not support Gregory's view and continued to teach that all the women disciples were representatives of the New Eve, the church and that Mary Magdalene joined with Mary, Jesus' mother, and John in Ephesus, to become martyrs.

Ironically, Pope Gregory's misinterpretation, which grew as only a good story can, made Mary Magdalene far more interesting especially to artists who, by the time of the Renaissance, were having a fine old time with half-naked women at the foot of the cross.

Legend after legend grew up around her. In one, she went into the desert to live as a hermit; French medieval tradition believed that Mary Magdalene was Mary of Bethany and that with her brother and sister,

Lazarus and Martha, sailed to Aix, in what is now France. Lazarus became the first Bishop of Marseilles, Martha defeated a dragon that was threatening the region, and Mary converted the king and queen of Southern Gaul to the new faith. The cult of Mary Magdalene spread across France, and relics of her body are alleged to be kept at many churches. This medieval legend assumed that she was a former prostitute, but had been redeemed through Christ.

This is the legend made popular by Margaret Starbird's novel *The Woman with the Alabaster Jar* (Bear & Co.) which writes of Mary's and Jesus's daughter, Sarah, becoming the founder of the Merovingian dynasty of French kings.

Mary's story inspires us today because she fills the vacant space of the Divine Feminine in the Protestant religion. We think that if she were so close to Jesus that she was the first to witness the resurrection, she must have been his lover or wife. But it is far more likely that she was his soul mate and that his destiny was inextricably entwined with hers.

CHAPTER ELEVEN

THE SACRED MARRIAGE

On the Sabbath Eve, that day in Bethany, there was no woman of the house to light the Sabbath lights. Simon was fully recovered from his leprosy and actively searching for a wife, having let the mother of his children go free when he contracted the disease but, for the moment, there were no women in his home.

Keturah, his wife of seventeen years, had been sorry, then relieved, having been granted permission to marry Simon's cousin. Simon and she were still friendly but she had her own house. They had no daughters and Simon had let the habit go; he had been too depressed and self-involved these last six years to worry about observing the Sabbath.

Often the men did it themselves; although the tradition was for the woman of the house they were staying at to welcome in the Sabbath, they were perfectly happy to do it themselves by calling on the Bride of Shabbat. Peter, Thomas, Judas and Andrew preferred it when there were no women present; they could never be comfortable juggling the purity laws and they simply didn't think that girls should be allowed in their group. But this night, particularly because he had invited Mary of Bethany to join them, together with her sister and brother, Yeshua was insistent that there should be a hostess.

Mary Magdalene was staying in a hostel nearby, together with Abigail. Joanna and Susannah were home in Jerusalem with their families so the choice was obvious. In any case, Yeshua wanted Mary's company; he found her laughter strengthening and he liked the fact that she did not always take him seriously. The disciples were always so very intense.

"I haven't done it very often," she confessed when he crossed the road to ask her to come. "I probably won't do it the way you are used to."

"That doesn't matter," he said. "My mother used to sing prayers beforehand and I loved that but, if that's not your way, then whatever you do will be perfect."

"She sang? Oh, my mother sang!" said Mary. "Not many people do nowadays."

"Do you remember the words?"

"Oh yes. You'll have to put up with my voice. It's a little like the warning horn at the harbour back home. You'll probably fall about laughing."

"All to the good," he said smiling.

"And it will be in Greek," she said, suddenly. "Not Aramaic. I don't know it in Aramaic."

"Any more excuses?" he said, leaning against the doorpost and staring up at the sky with one eyebrow raised and a smile on his lips.

"You rascal!" she said, feigning a slap to the side of his head. "Have some respect for your elders!"

"Why?" he said, dodging, a broad grin illuminating his face. "Just because you're old doesn't make you wise. It certainly doesn't make you witty!"

"That remark will cost you your bread at supper," she said. "I shall eat it in front of you, savouring every last morsel while you whimper."

"You can't," he said. "I'm the one breaking the bread for Shabbat. I won't give you any then!"

"Then Shekhinah will pass you by," she retorted with a toss of her head and a giggle. "Because she'll see how very unkind you are."

"Unfair!" he cried.

"Childish!" she replied. "If you can't keep up with your elders, don't play!"

They both laughed; feeling such a kinship; such connection; such a relief to have a friend with whom they could laugh. Neither could explain it exactly – but both hoped to feel it again.

So, at dusk, she stood before the two candles, in Simon's house, remembering back to her childhood and the times when her mother had told her the stories of Shekhinah and how the great goddess would fly to the heart of any woman who blessed the Sabbath. How many years now? Too many to mention. The male disciples were restless, waiting for her to start but the two new women looked at her longingly; they probably envy me, she thought wryly. If only they knew how nervous I am. She closed her eyes and concentrated, remembering the prayer.

This is what she sang, as women the world over have sung for more than 2000 years:

Lord of the Universe, I am about to perform the sacred duty of kindling the lights in honor of the Sabbath. Even as it is written: 'And Thou shalt call the Sabbath a delight and the holy day of the Lord honorable.'

"And may the effect of my fulfilling this commandment be that the stream of abundant life and heavenly blessing flow in upon me and mine. That Thou be gracious unto us and cause thy presence to dwell among us.

"Father of mercy, O continue thy loving kindness unto me and unto my dear ones. Make me worthy to (rear my children that they) walk in the way of the righteous before thee, loyal to thy law and clinging to good deeds. Keep Thou far from us all manner of shame, grief and care and grant that peace, light and joy ever abide in our home. For with thee is the fountain of life; in thy light do we see light. Amen."

As she lit the candles she felt the cascade of light and strength pour into her very bones. She knew who she was; why she was; how she was and, at last, that she had a purpose. She knew, at last, that she was home. That was her first experience of the Sacred Marriage, the inner union of heaven and earth.

Mary was Yeshua's elder by five years. Maybe she did fall a little in love with him and he with her but it is hard to tell the difference between sacred and sexual love; both carry a charge that lifts hearts and shines through the eyes. It's most likely that there was never anything sexual in those feelings; neither was looking for a physical relationship. Peter was physically more the kind of man that Mary liked but even if he hadn't had a wife back home in Capernaum, that was never going to happen. Peter thought she was the spawn of Satan for her arrogance and the fact that she actually knew what his teacher was talking about when he struggled to understand.

She teased Peter for a while, once she was confident of her place in that group and found herself able to interpret what Yeshua had to say in what she called "common terms for the common people". Their Rabbi had spent too long at school in the Temple not to use words that made them all feel stupid at times, she thought. It was better when he told stories, but even those were hard to interpret. But teasing Simon Peter was not a good idea. He went red in the face and his outbursts of anger were scalding. He was best left to simmer for placating him did no good either.

Instead, she turned her focus onto Yeshua because that brought joy; the fire of the passion of Divine Love between them made it hard for the others to tell what was going on. It made both men and women jealous but only because they could not reach the heights that Jesus was constantly trying to teach them to reach. Maybe some of the other women did; it was the secret of experiencing the Shekhinah and that, traditionally, is the role of the feminine. Mary of Bethany understood – but at the cost of angering her sister Martha who grumbled and muttered while she did the cooking and Mary sat listening to the Rabbi. Martha could not understand that the dinner could wait an hour; that no one noticed the dust on the windowsill. She wanted the teacher to work to her schedule and he did not seem to work to any schedule at all.

Sometimes Mary talked with Yeshua about Tamar, about Sarah, about his father. Sometimes she told him about her husband and son. He told her that Tamar would have liked her but, secretly, she doubted it. Wives and husbands rarely like spiritual companions; they are a far greater threat than a strumpet for they have a place in the soul. His mother, she knew, thought her loud and unladylike but they could make each other laugh and, after some initial animal circling and chaffing at each other, they made peace. The other Miriam was wise and holy, Mary could see that. She envied the older woman her peace of mind and, once she had said so, the final veil was broken between them. Sometimes Yeshua would find them together, talking or with one of them lying with her head in the other's lap. They were the two he went to for his own peace and there were times when he slept, exhausted, in Mary's arms; the most precious burden to hold and to cherish. She knew she was the luckiest woman on Earth.

When he was taken and he died, Salome, his sister, Mary of Bethany and Mary Magdalene waited outside the tomb. They did not fight the authorities; they did not campaign to get his name cleared; they did not build a cairn in his remembrance; they did not try to teach in his place; they did not shout about how wrong it was, how unfair. They did not deny him. They sat and waited because they felt an inner peace that could not be described. They did not need to be active or fierce.

And they had their reward.

Partners on the path

Their story truly begins once Jesus' story had ended. What did they do with their lives after such an experience? We can never know; they didn't write it down. And neither have hundreds of thousands of men and women who have also experienced the Divine while living on Earth both before and afterward.

Sacred Marriage is union between the self and with God. It is depicted as being something only for the very holy but the intention of Holy Scripture is to demonstrate that it is available to us every day of our lives. Jesus called it the Kingdom of God, others call it communion, Kundalini rising, Tantra and many other names. It can be accessed both with a partner, either with and without sexual union, and alone. God Itself has no sex, being absolute and ineffable, but union with the Divine is often easier to attempt when the masculine or feminine aspects of God are addressed either in the physical and psychological worlds or by focusing on the aspect of God that is the opposite of your own sex.

This helps explain the Roman Catholic priest's adoration of the Virgin; she is Shekhinah and he is the male consort. Union between the two will lift the man to the level of Christhood. In the same way, for a woman, union with the masculine Christ figure lifts her to the same level. Nuns are traditionally called Brides of Christ. Mystics understand the Christhood to be a spiritual level which is both simultaneously within and without us – immanent and transcendent. Although Christ is a title usually only given to Jesus, it is not unique to one person, rather the goal of all humanity. Kabbalah teaches that every human soul will, one day, be Christed; this is the whole purpose of creation. When we are all Christ, then the Divine Plan will be complete.

But religion, as opposed to spirituality, does not teach this. Instead of making Jesus, Buddha, Mohammad, Krishna and other Christed beings the way-showers and taking the journey they are showing us, we focus on them. We worship the signpost instead of undertaking the journey.

Many Gnostics take the view that Jesus of Nazareth never existed – that he is the personification of an inner human need for the Divine rather than a physical human who achieved this on Earth. The word *Gnostic* comes from the Greek word *gnosis,* or knowledge, but being used in the sense of direct experience. But if Jesus didn't walk this earth how can we aspire to be as he was? If he were wholly Divine and not a human creature we can never be as good as he and that is the great spiritual cop-out that has beset Christianity for centuries.

In the introduction to his *The Original New Testament* (Element), Jewish scholar, Hugh Schonfield writes: "the Bible is not so much about Man's theology as God's anthropology." Schonfield's many books pull apart the Jesus legend; his *Passover Plot* (Element) is one of several works by different authors that affirm that Jesus did not die on the cross at all. So we have two schools of thought: one, that Jesus was wholly human and the whole Christian story is a farce and the other, that Jesus was wholly Divine and we must worship him and accept that he and only he is the physical representation of God.

It is easy to get lost in either theory but really the point is our own spiritual journey and how we can best support ourselves on our way. If we take the middle line that Jesus (like many others) was a human who could access the Divine and showed us the way to do the same, we can get a lot further. Conspiracy theories are time-consuming distractions just as are the views that Jesus and Mary are gods and not human at all.

Exactly the same imposition of divinity happened to Jesus' mother as did to him; she has become perceived as being more and more holy and less and less human. The Virgin Mary, perpetual virgin, born without sin, never dirtied a hand in the realities of Earth. It got to the stage where she couldn't have a body rotting in the earth either because that would mean she was corruptible, so she was ruled to have been bodily assumed into heaven. This using of Mary as an interpretation of Shekhinah is both useful in showing us the perfect Divine feminine and a great disservice in demonising sexuality and the perceived evils of the feminine, particularly shown through the female's tempting of Adam to eat the fruit of the Tree of Knowledge.

It is very human to create gods. Terry Pratchett's novel *Small Gods* (Corgi) describes the process exactly. In it, the formerly great god Om who could once smite cities is reduced to the size and power of a tortoise because his religion has become more important than he is. No one believes in Om any more, they just believe in the rules and regulations.

Jews regard Christianity as a pagan religion which breaks the second commandment: "Thou shalt not make unto thee any graven image, or any likeness in heaven above, or in the earth beneath, or in the water under the earth. Thou shalt not bow down thyself to them, nor serve them." (Exodus 4:24). A graven image is one that is unchangeable, carved in stone, and therefore is not open to any other interpretation –the image of God as an old man, for example, or the image of Christ as just one human being.

Most fundamentalist views of Christianity take John's Gospel as the only truth, making it a graven image. The Kabbalistic interpretation, as we have seen, is that each of the Gospels has its own level and John's is the level of the Divine world. This world is transpersonal, beyond the physical, and therefore its interpretation of Jesus is indeed of almost cosmic consciousness. My studies of Kabbalah would indicate that this was intended to be read as a personal meditation of the Christ within all of us. To read the Gospel with one's self in the place of Jesus is an extraordinary experience and the swiftest path to understanding the Sacred Marriage that exists in the Christian teachings.

What is more, it is a pathway open to every person who can read for themselves. A clue here is that the great "I am" pronouncements of Christianity, which are used to exclude those who are not wholehearted believers in Christ as God, are given in a slightly different form than when Jesus says phrases such as "I am thirsty" (*dipseo*) or

"I am come" (*erchomai*) where the "I" usage of the verb is all that is required. Or even from the usage in phrases such as "I am meek" (Matthew 11:29) where there is a subject and an object and Jesus uses the word "*eimi*" which means "I am." For the great pronouncements such as: "I am the resurrection, and the life: he that believeth in me, though he were dead, yet shall he live." (John 11:25), he notably uses two words for I, *ego, eimi*. This can be construed to mean emphasis, "I, myself". But for the mystic it is a direct reference to the great name of God as given to Moses in Exodus:

"And God said unto Moses, I AM THAT I AM: and he said, Thus shalt thou say unto the children of Israel, I AM hath sent me unto you." (Exodus 3:14). When Jesus says the words with such emphasis, he is saying the great I AM – that the consciousness of the Christ within is the resurrection and the life; the way, the truth and the life. The phrase "he that believeth in me" can equally mean "he that believes in the Christ within".

Moses' experience with God at the Burning Bush in Exodus is an excellent example of the Sacred Marriage where the Divine is merged with the human. Moses' initiation can be demonstrated through the Kabbalistic Tree of Life or through the Hindu Chakras with God as the Crown Chakra, the Burning Bush as the Third Eye (clairvoyance), the voice of the angel as the Throat Chakra (clairaudience), Moses himself as the Heart Chakra (the link between heaven and earth – the Kingdom of Heaven), Pharaoh as the Solar Plexus Chakra (the Self – also the level of pride), the Egyptians as the Gonadic Chakra (the Ego) and the Israelites as the Base Chakra (basic life and survival).

Sacred Marriage

When all the human energy centres are aligned and open then the Sacred Marriage can occur. This sometimes happens during sexual orgasm which is probably the original reason why it has been used in many spiritual practices for centuries – and one of the reasons why sexuality is so frightening to the celibate. Sexuality is also a wonderful distraction from the spiritual search. Why look for God when you can get equivalent pleasure in sex?

As well as Sacred Marriage there is soul marriage and many times it is the help of the partner that lifts the seeking soul to be able to achieve Sacred Marriage. A bad marriage is an incredible impediment to spiritual growth but the challenge is to transform it rather than destroy it.

It is the same with the human ego; so much of what is taught as doctrine (in all religions) is ego rather than truth. Ego is the part of us which believes in duality and which must be proved to be right. The Self with a capital S is strong enough to allow others to have valid views; the ego must be shown to be right and, if anyone has a differing opinion, then they must be wrong. The ego is dissolved at death and at the moment of Sacred Marriage; this is a transformation where it is merged with the soul and understands the concept of unity but for most of us, the thought of losing the ego – our personal self – is terrifying. Far better to create a religion with a built-in failure device where we are unable to emulate the Divine. The human ego has been kept under control by religion for centuries (although many of the religious leaders themselves were ruled by their own egos). Nowadays, in the secular world, it is sex, money and possessions which keep it too busy to be interested in seeking God.

Ultimately, the Sacred Marriage is the goal of all seekers of Christ/God – the merging of heaven and earth. The Greek philosopher Plotinus called it "the flight of the Alone to the Alone," the utmost bliss of the emancipated soul. St Theresa of Avila and Hildegard of Bingham both wrote of it. St Theresa was a Carmelite nun who lived between 1515 and 1582 and who regularly spent hours in meditation which she called the prayer of quiet or the prayer of union. During these times she frequently went into a trance, and took mystical flights in which she would feel as if her soul were lifted out of her body. She said this ecstasy was like a "detachable death" where her soul became awake to God as never before. Her first book, *Life*, written in 1565, describes how she experienced a spiritual marriage with Christ as bridegroom to the soul. *The Interior Castle* (1577) is her best-known work, where she teaches spiritual doctrine using a castle to symbolize the interior life. St Theresa's physical helper or soul-mate was the Carmelite monk, St John of the Cross.

St Augustine wrote of the Sacred Marriage in his *Confesssions:*

"I entered into the secret closet of my soul, led by Thee; and this I could do because Thou wast my helper. I entered, and beheld with the mysterious eye of my soul the Light that never changes, above the eye of my soul, above my intelligence. It was not the common light which all flesh can see, nor was it greater yet of the same kind, as if the light of day were to grow brighter and brighter and flood all space. It was not like this, but different: altogether different from all such things."

And St Hildegarde of Bingen wrote in an extract from her poetry:

"I am the supreme fiery force
That kindles every spark of life;
What I have breathed on will never die...
I am divine fiery life..."

We can achieve spiritual union whether or not we live celibate lives – but we must embrace the concepts of masculine and feminine that are at its heart. The spiritual union between God and Israel is expressed in Exodus 19:17 by the idea of Moses being the "friend of the bridegroom" who leads out the bride (Israel) and in psalm 68:7 Jehovah as the bridegroom meets his Church at Sinai.

Anne Baring, co-author with Andrew Harvey of *The Divine Feminine* (Godsfield Press) says that without the concept of Sacred Marriage within ourselves we split nature and matter (perceived as feminine) from spirit (perceived as masculine) leading to rationality and the rule of science. This making of the feminine evil is what allows us to pollute and misuse what we still term Mother Earth.

Nature, woman and body were seen as what had to be conquered, controlled, made subject, because instinct within and nature without were perceived as chaotic, overwhelmingly powerful and threatening. Is it surprising then that, ultimately, Mother Earth, nature and matter should come to be regarded as something mindless and mechanical – to be exploited, dominated and controlled as we choose?

A soul partnership between two people, such as Mary and Jesus, whose lives are intertwined for some great purpose, does not have to involve a sexual relationship; in fact sex is quite often the furthest thing from such people's minds. In Kabbalah it is taught that we humans operate on several different levels including vegetable, animal and human. The vegetable level is the one concerned with food, comfort, sex, children and safety; the animal level with our position in the tribe and issues of power; and the human level is concerned with soul-development.

It is said, in the mystery schools, that when a being of great destiny comes to fulfil his or her life, there is always a soul mate – perhaps even a twin soul – to work with them as their help and support. That soul mate does not even have to be the same sex. For Moses, it might have been his brother Aaron, his sister Miriam or his wife Zipporah. For King David it might have been Jonathan, Abishag the Shunammite who warmed his heart in his old age or even King Saul. For Queen Esther it might have been Mordecai or her husband Ahasuerus.

This relationship, however it is structured is the help and strength that enables the Anointed One to do his or her work in the world. Sometimes the union of the two is what lifts them to the higher consciousness needed but, more often, there is a mutually-fulfilling four-way relationship. The spiritual seekers both have a sacred covenant with God as well as acting as support for each other.

Whether or not Jesus of Nazareth was married, to accept the idea that Jesus was a totally non-sexual being is to take away a vital part of his humanity. The only way he can be an icon, a window to the celestial worlds, is for him to have been one of us as well as the Divine on Earth. That means that we too can aspire to be the same.

Those who are called to be celibate take a worthy path with great challenges and blessings, not least the question of whether or not they are avoiding engagement with the full joys of life. The Talmud states clearly that humanity will be called to account for having deprived itself of any of the good things which the world offers (*Kiddushin* end). To promote the idea that celibacy is a superior path to God is therefore more like a declaration of war than an affirmation of the Kingdom of God.

Where there is duality, as there is on Earth, there must also be both God and Goddess. Where there is unity – as in the Godhead Itself – there is no division; no disharmony; no distinction; no condemnation of the opposite.

When the male and the female come together, there is the Divine Child. That child is present in all of us, just as it was in Tamar, in Eve and in both the Marys. If Jesus were the Anointed One of his age, he would have known that and embraced it.

As he would have known and embraced his wife.

BOOKS

O books
O is a symbol of the world, of oneness and unity. In different cultures it also means the "eye", symbolizing knowledge and insight, and in Old English it means "place of love or home". O books explores the many paths of understanding which different traditions have developed down the ages, particularly those today that express respect for the planet and all of life.

For more information on the full list of over 300 titles please visit our website
www.O-books.net

myspiritradio is an exciting web, internet, podcast and mobile phone global broadcast network for all those interested in teaching and learning in the fields of body, mind, spirit and self development. Listeners can hear the show online via computer or mobile phone, and even download their favourite shows to listen to on MP3 players whilst driving, working, or relaxing.

Feed your mind, change your life with O Books, The O Books radio programme carries inter-views with most authors, sharing their wisdom on life, the universe and everything...e mail questions and co-create the show with O Books and myspiritradio.

mySpiritRadio

Just visit **www.myspiritradio.com** for more information.

Censored Messiah
The truth about Jesus Christ
Peter Cresswell

This revolutionary theory about the life of Jesus and the origins of Christianity describes his role in the Nazorean movement, linked to the Essenes and other contemporary groups opposed to Roman rule- one that reflected the tensions between active revolt and the expectation for divine deliverance. The gospels do provide narrative and an explanation for something that really happened, but were censored and edited by later followers after the destruction of Jerusalem to disguise Jesus' Jewish roots an protect sources.

190381667X 248pp £9.99 $14.95

The Gay Disciple
Jesus' friend tells it his own way
John Henson

John offers the reflective reader a perspective on incidents and characters which at the very least make one think and which often help sharpen ones perception of what was, or might have been, going on. He manages to combine the strengths of the Sunday papers columnist approach with the radical evangelical message delivery of one who invites you to think! **Meic Phillips** ONE co-ordinator

184694001X 128pp £9.99 $19.95

The Laughing Jesus
Religious lies and Gnostic wisdom
Timothy Freke and Peter Gandy

The Laughing Jesus is a manifesto for Gnostic mysticism. Freke and Gandy's exposition of Gnostic enlightenment is lucid and accessible; their

critique of Literalist religion is damningly severe. **Robert M. Price**, Professor of scriptural studies, editor of *The Journal of Higher Criticism* 1905047819 272pp **£9.99** UK and Commonwealth rights only

The Creative Christian
God and us; Partners in Creation
Adrian B. Smith

Enlivening and stimulating, the author presents a new approach to Jesus and the Kingdom he spoke of, in the context of the evolution of our Universe. He reveals its meaning for us of the 21st century. **Hans Schrenk**, Lecturer in Holy Scripture and Biblical Languages, Middlesex University. 1905047754 144pp **£11.99 $24.95**

The Gospel of Falling Down
Mark Townsend

Humble, searching, faith-filled, and yet risky and creative at the same time. **Richard Rohr** OFM

This little book is tackling one of the biggest and deepest questions which, unexpectedly, brings us to the foundation of the Christian faith. Mark has discovered this through his own experience of falling down, or failure. **Bishop Stephen Verney**
1846940095 144pp £9.99 $16.95

I Still Haven't Found What I'm Looking For
Paul Walker

Traditional understandings of Christianity may not be credible but they can still speak to us in a different way. They point to something which we can still sense. Something we need in our lives. Something not just to make us decent, or responsible, but happy and fulfilled. Paul Walker, former *Times* Preacher of the Year, rejoices in the search.
1905047762 144pp **£9.99 $16.95**

An Introduction to Radical Theology
The death and resurrection of God
Trevor Greenfield

This is a clearly written and scholarly introduction to radical theology that, at the same time, provides a contextualised and much needed survey of the movement. At times and in turns Greenfield is passionate, ironical, polemical and acerbic. A significant and valuable addition to the literature. **Journal of Beliefs and Values**
1905047606 208pp £12.99 $29.95

Tomorrow's Christian
A new framework for Christian living
Adrian B. Smith

This is a vision of a radically new kind of Christianity. While many of the ideas here have been accepted by radical Christians and liberal theologians for some time, this presents them as an accessible, coherent package: a faith you can imagine living out with integrity in the real world. And even if you already see yourself as a "progressive Christian" or whatever label you choose to adopt, you'll find ideas in both books that challenge and surprise you. Highly recommended. **Movement**
1903816971 176pp £9.99 $15.95

Tomorrow's Faith
A new framework of Christian belief
Adrian B. Smith
2nd printing

This is the most significant book for Christian thinking so far this millennium. If this does not become a standard textbook for theological and ministerial education, then shame on the institutions! **Revd Dr Meic Phillips**, Presbyterian
1905047177 128pp £9.99 $19.95

The Trouble With God
Building the republic of heaven
David Boulton
Revised edition

A wonderful repository of religious understanding and a liberal theologian's delight. **Modern Believing**

Lively and stimulating, a crusading zeal imbued with both historical perspective and a bracing, unsentimental determination to assert that human spirituality, in all its fullness of transcendent potential, is sufficient to redeem us from the despair of nihilism and the banality of evil. **Universalist**
1905047061 272pp **£11.99 $24.95**

Back to the Truth
5,000 years of Advaita
Dennis Waite

A wonderful book. Encyclopedic in nature, and destined to become a classic. **James Braha**

Absolutely brilliant…an ease of writing with a water-tight argument outlining the great universal truths. This book will become a modern classic. A milestone in the history of Advaita. **Paula Marvelly**
1905047614 500pp **£19.95 $29.95**

Beyond Photography
Encounters with orbs, angels and mysterious light forms
Katie Hall and John Pickering

The authors invite you to join them on a fascinating quest; a voyage of discovery into the nature of a phenomenon, manifestations of which are shown as being historical and global as well as contemporary and intently personal.

At journey's end you may find yourself a believer, a doubter or simply an intrigued wonderer… Whatever the outcome, the process of journeying is likely prove provocative and stimulating and - as with the mysterious

images fleetingly captured by the authors' cameras - inspiring and potentially enlightening. **Brian Sibley**, author and broadcaster.
1905047908 272pp 50 b/w photos +8pp colour insert **£12.99 $24.95**

Don't Get MAD Get Wise
Why no one ever makes you angry, ever!
Mike George
There is a journey we all need to make, from anger, to peace, to forgiveness. Anger always destroys, peace always restores, and forgiveness always heals. This explains the journey, the steps you can take to make it happen for you.
1905047827 160pp **£7.99 $14.95**

IF You Fall...
It's a new beginning
Karen Darke
Karen Darke's story is about the indomitability of spirit, from one of life's cruel vagaries of fortune to what is insight and inspiration. She has overcome the limitations of paralysis and discovered a life of challenge and adventure that many of us only dream about. It is all about the mind, the spirit and the desire that some of us find, but which all of us possess. **Joe Simpson**, mountaineer and author of *Touching the Void*
1905047886 240pp £9.99 $19.95

Love, Healing and Happiness
Spiritual wisdom for a post-secular era
Larry Culliford
This will become a classic book on spirituality. It is immensely practical and grounded. It mirrors the author's compassion and lays the foundation for a higher understanding of human suffering and hope. **Reinhard Kowalski** Consultant Clinical Psychologist
1905047916 304pp **£10.99 $19.95**

A Map to God
Awakening Spiritual Integrity
Susie Anthony

This describes an ancient hermetic pathway, representing a golden thread running through many traditions, which offers all we need to understand and do to actually become our best selves.

1846940443 260pp **£10.99 $21.95**

Punk Science
Inside the mind of God
Manjir Samanta-Laughton

Wow! Punk Science is an extraordinary journey from the microcosm of the atom to the macrocosm of the Universe and all stops in between. Manjir Samanta-Laughton's synthesis of cosmology and consciousness is sheer genius. It is elegant, simple and, as an added bonus, makes great reading.
Dr Bruce H. Lipton, author of *The Biology of Belief*

1905047932 320pp **£12.95 $22.95**

Rosslyn Revealed
A secret library in stone
Alan Butler

Rosslyn Revealed gets to the bottom of the mystery of the chapel featured in the Da Vinci Code. The results of a lifetime of careful research and study demonstrate that truth really is stranger than fiction; a library of philosophical ideas and mystery rites, that were heresy in their time, have been disguised in the extraordinarily elaborate stone carvings.

1905047924 260pp b/w + colour illustrations **£19.95 $29.95** cl